ANDRE THOMKINS   PERMANENTSZENE

ANDRE THOMKINS

PERMANENTSZENE

Zeichnungen, Aquarelle, Bilder, Collagen,
Objecte und Texte von 1946–1977

Drawings, Watercolours, Paintings, Collages,
Objects and Texts from 1946–1977

edition hansjörg mayer   stuttgart london

published 1978   edition hansjörg mayer
engelhornweg 11   d-7 stuttgart 1   germany

edition of 4000
printed by staib + mayer   stuttgart   germany

photographs of the artist by
rudi meisel and kees broos
photographs of the objects by nicolas thomkins

content

-türst und sträggelen-   andré Thomkins   1977

– Kleine Bogenschützen –   André Tromterus 1953

— herr rohrschack —   andré thomkins
                                                            1961

14

André Dressikius
1944
Bacchanale à sang sec —

15

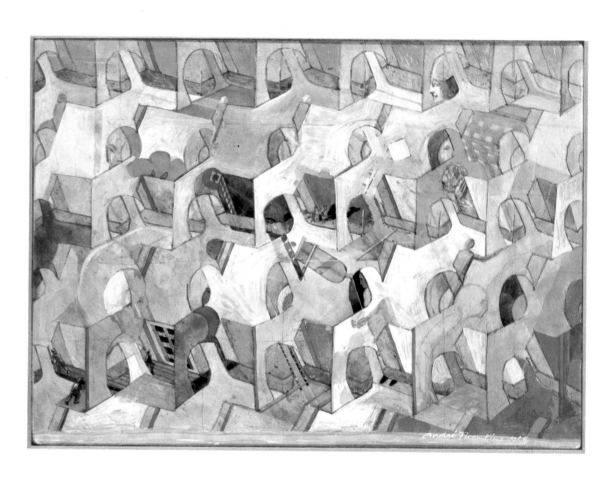

- Klosterberg -

ANDRÉ THOMKINS
1969

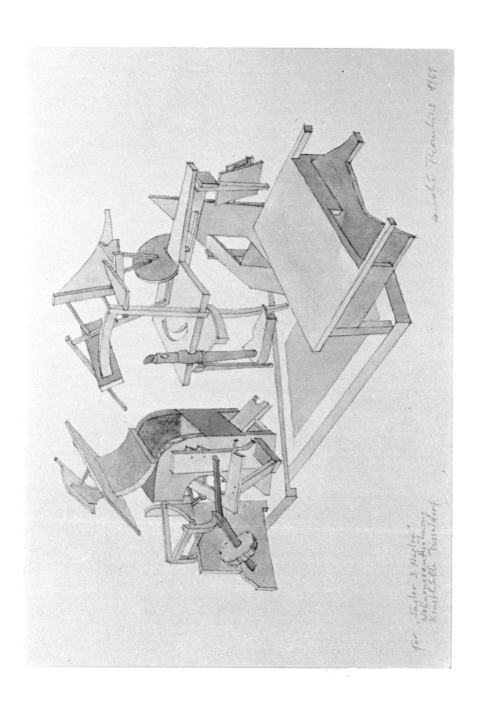

20

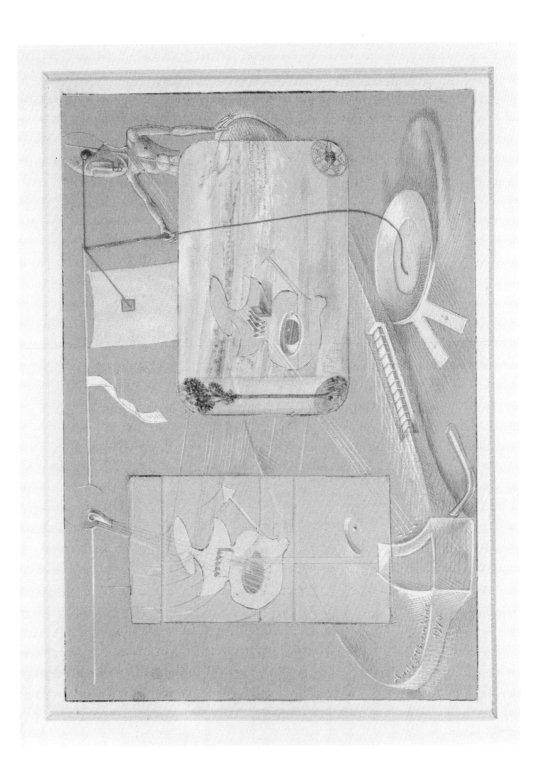

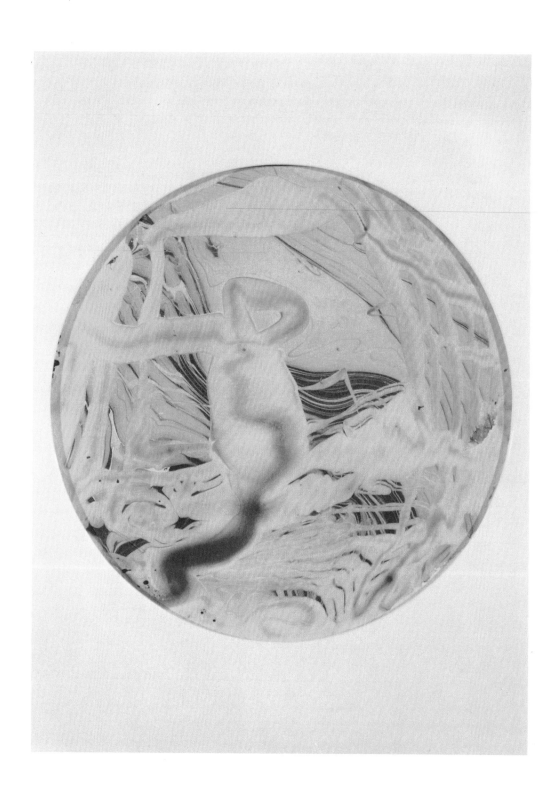

die jahrhundert-
wender

André Thomkins
1970

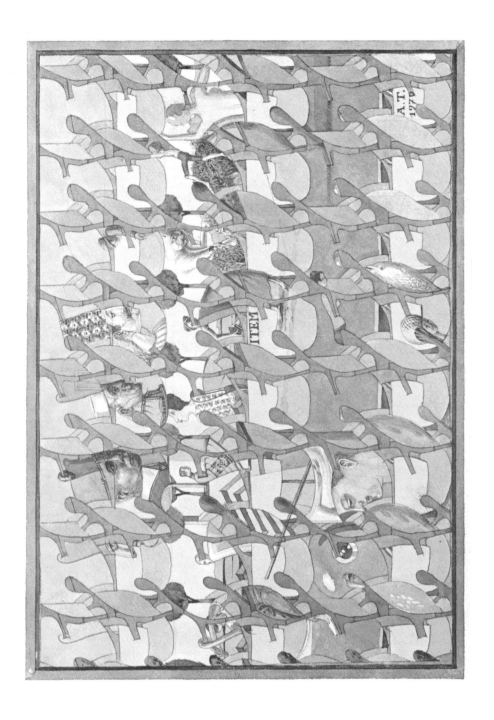

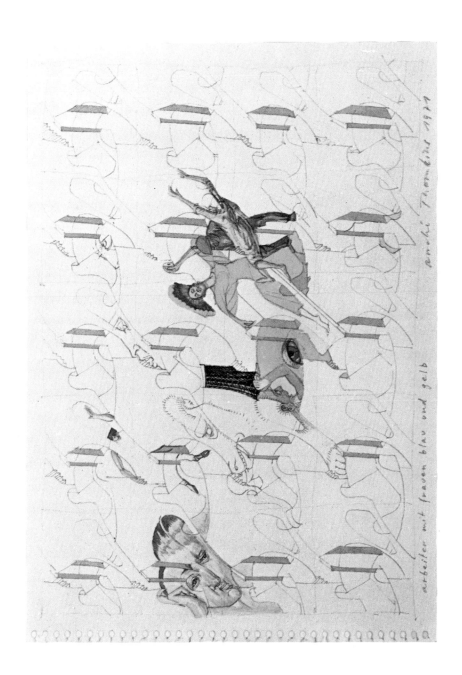

arbeiter mit frauen blau und gelb   André Thomkins 1977

25

KNESSET
1971
ANDRE THOMKINS
pro figlia Jenison T.

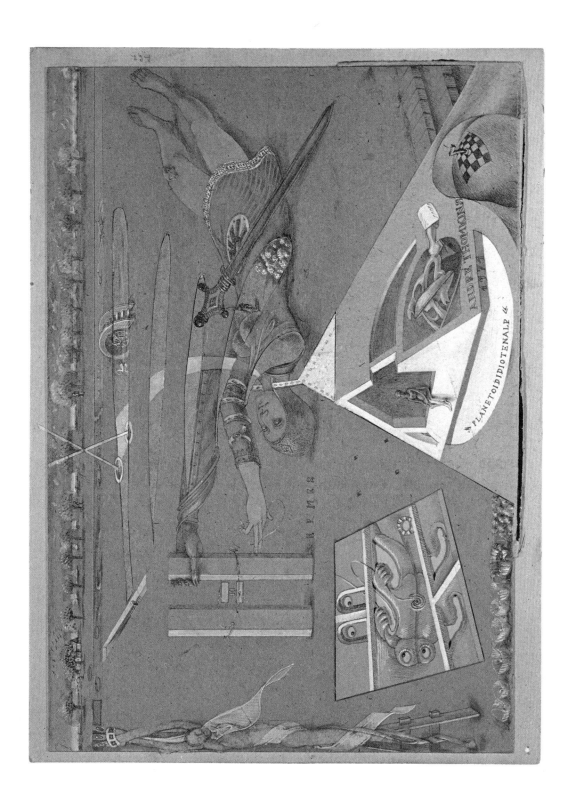

27

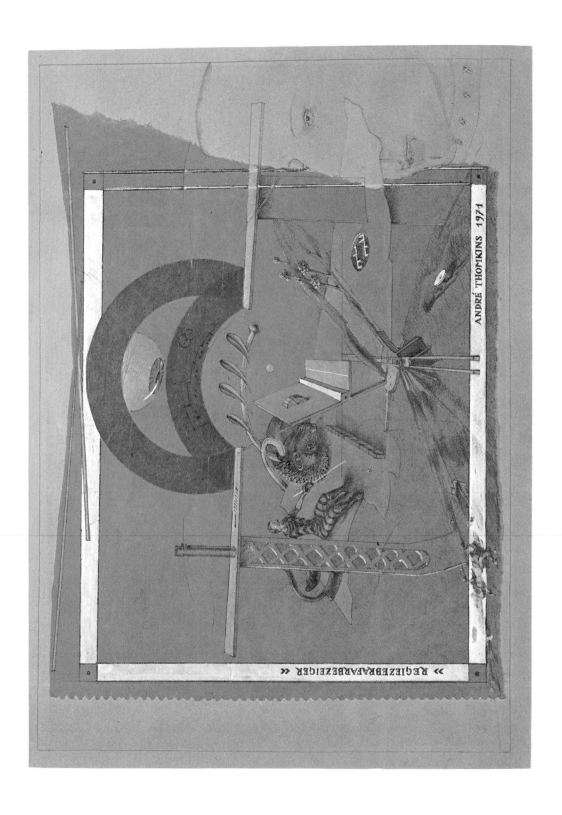

ANDRÉ THOMKINS 1974

» REGIEZEBRAFARBEZEIGER «

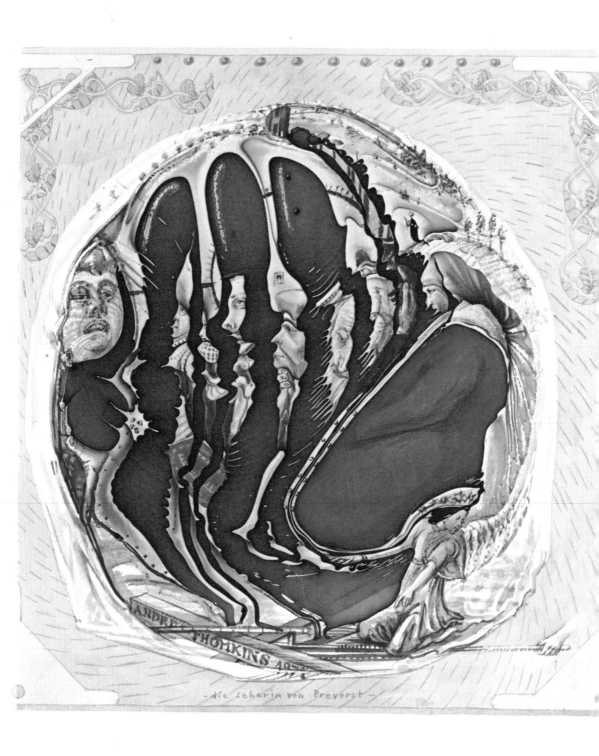

ANDREAS THOMKINS 195.

— die Seherin von Prevorst —

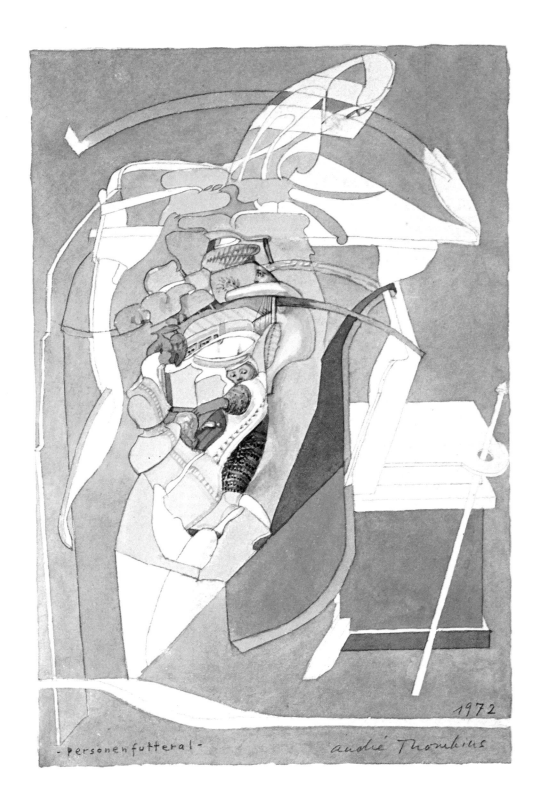

- personenfutteral -

1972

andré Thomkins

31

colli Euganei   G. Thombres 1972

mei Tingen

PADOVANE A. T. 72

35

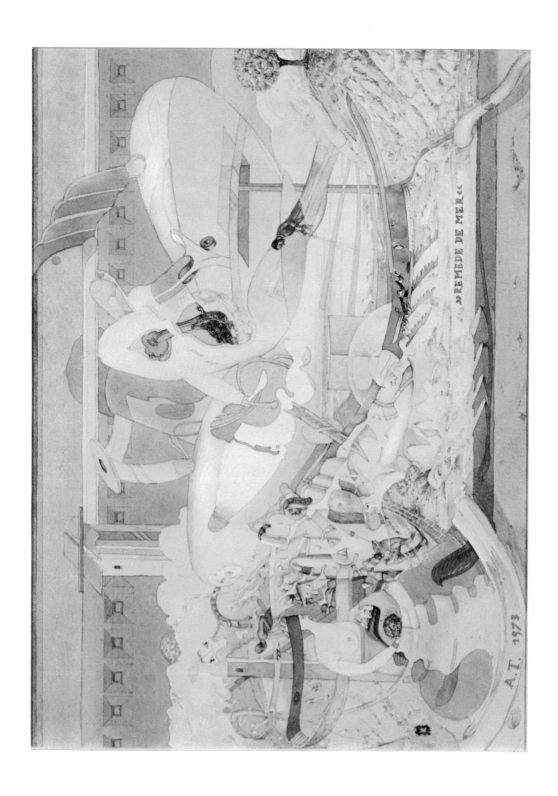

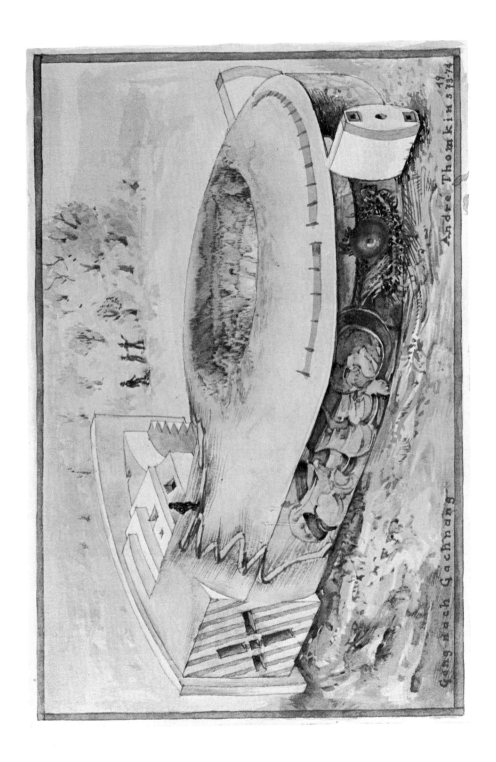

Gang nach Gachnang

André Thomkins 73-74

les Entrelacs à Interlaken – 1975
André Thomkins

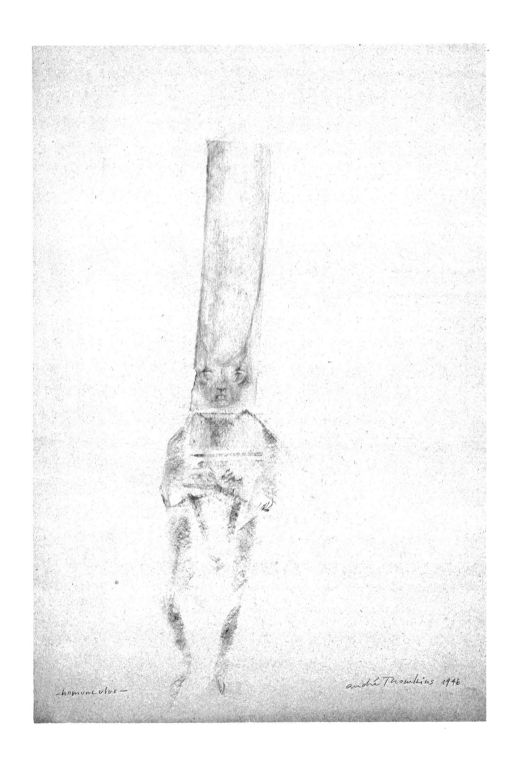

−homunculus−   andré Thomkins 1946

André Rosenbühns, 1977

André Thouless 1948

— cerberus —

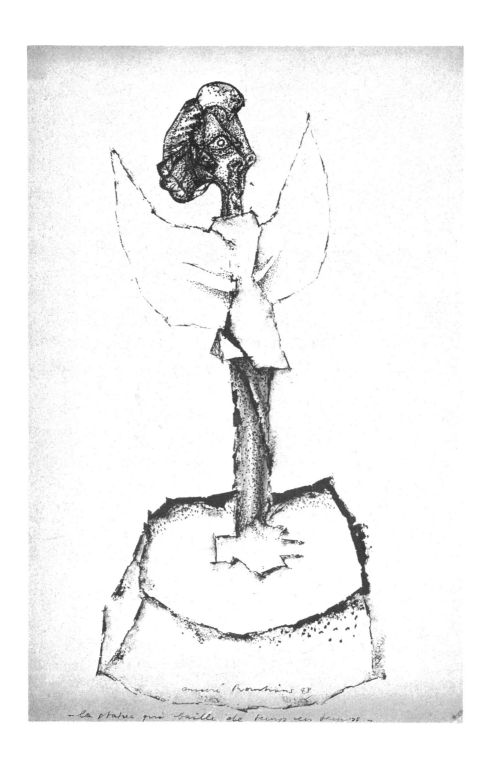

— la statue qui baille de temps en temps —

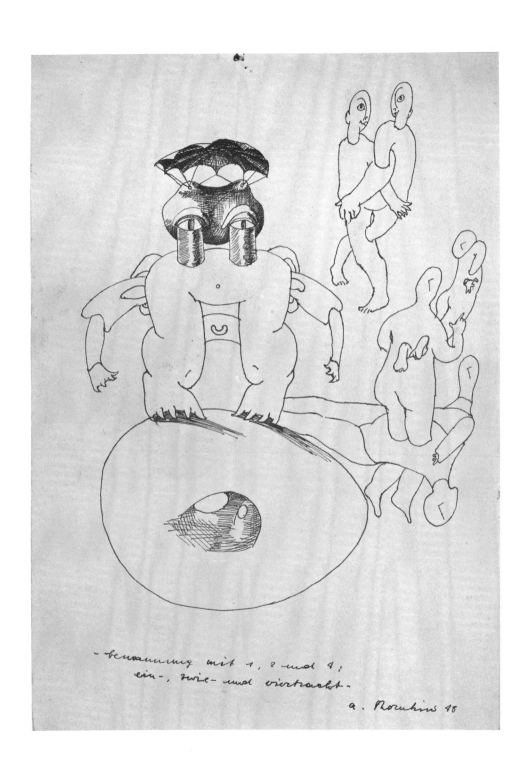

- benennung mit 1, 2 und 4;
  ein-, zwie- und viertracht.

a. Rozumira 48

47

grandpapa

andré Thomkins 1949

48

Kopfstudien.   andré Thomkins 1949.

49

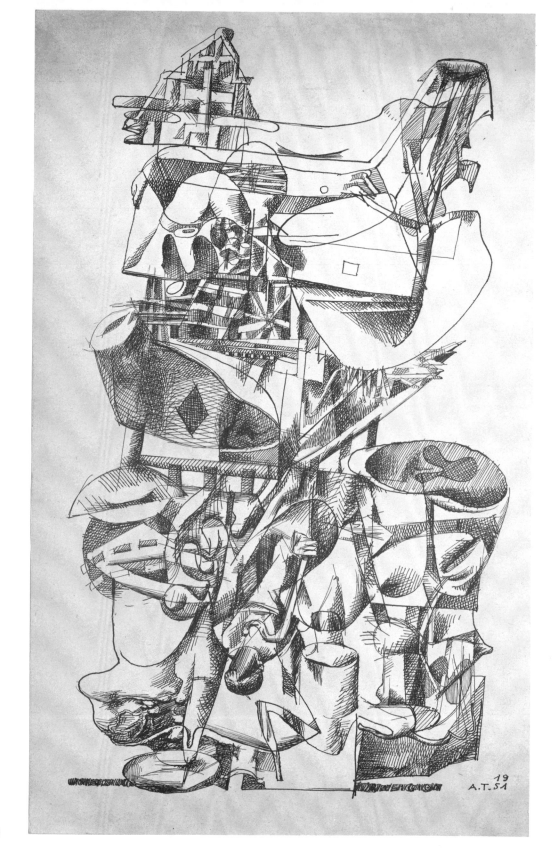

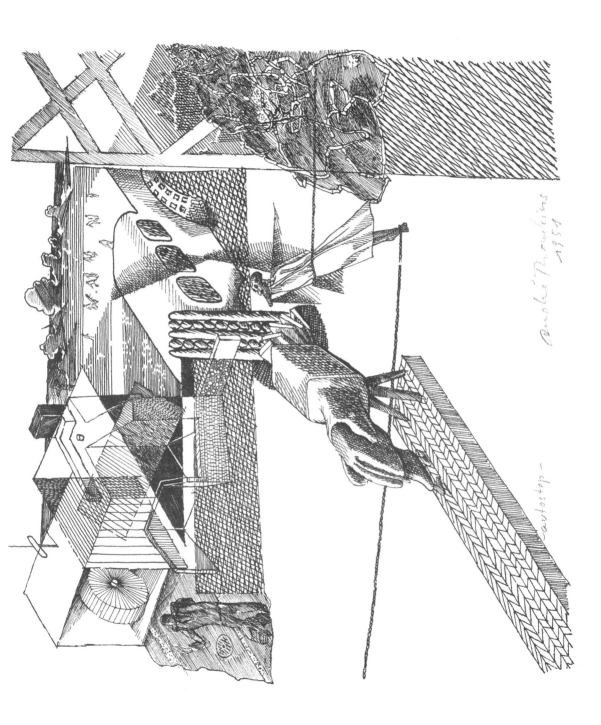

autostop –

Amália Zirombirons
1954

51

André Thankers 1952

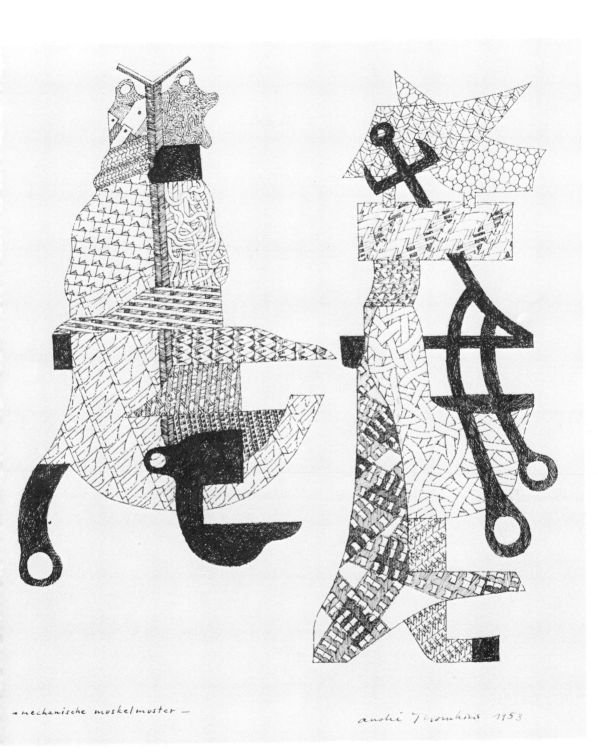

» mechanische muskelmuster –

andré Thomkins 1953

53

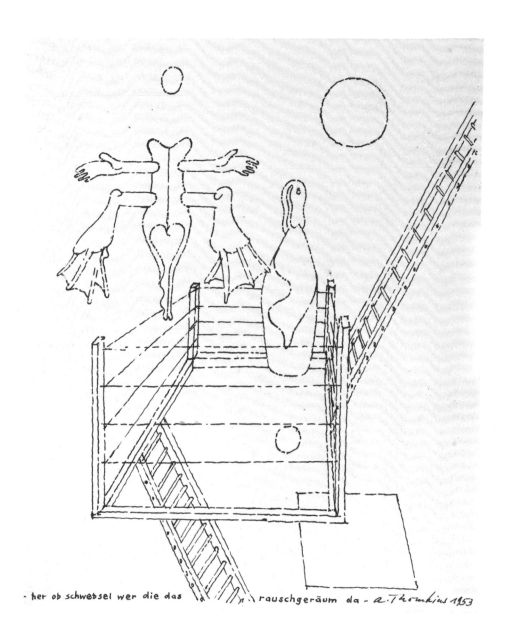

- her ob schwebsel wer die das rauschgeräum da - a. Thomkins 1953

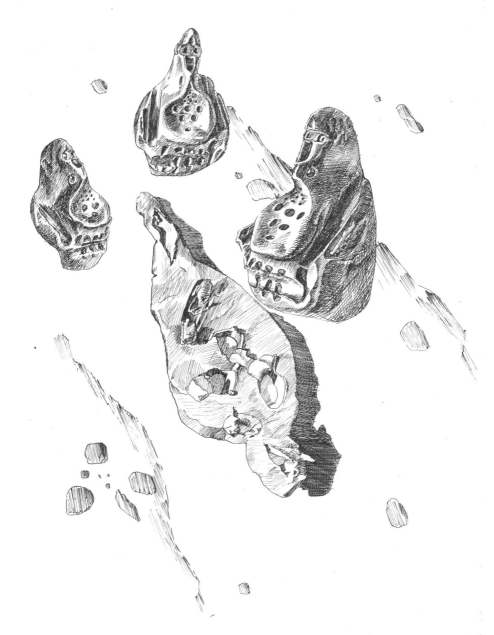

andré Thomkins 1954   er hat das steinerbliche gesegnet

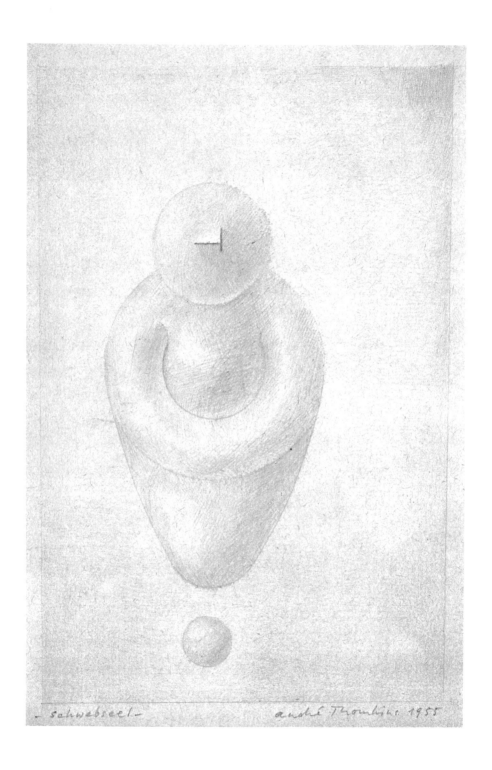

- schwebseel -

andré Thomkins 1955

56

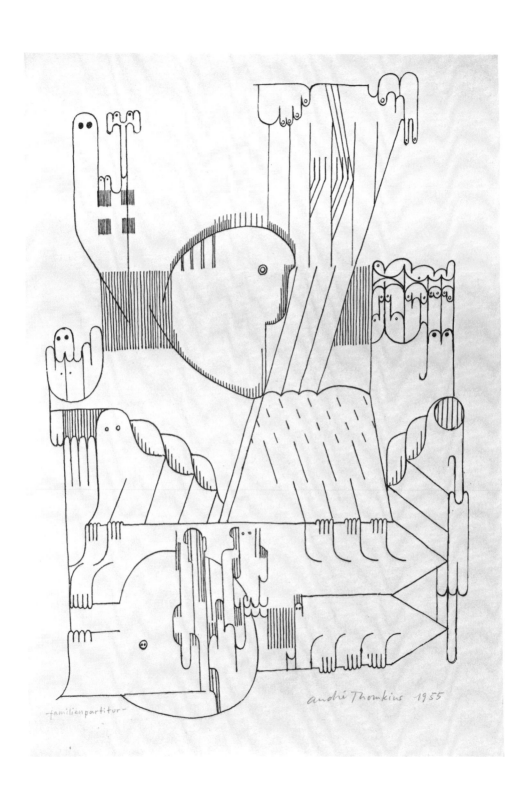

- familienpartitur -

andré Thomkins 1955

- Wirbelwüchsige -

andré Thomkins 1955

58

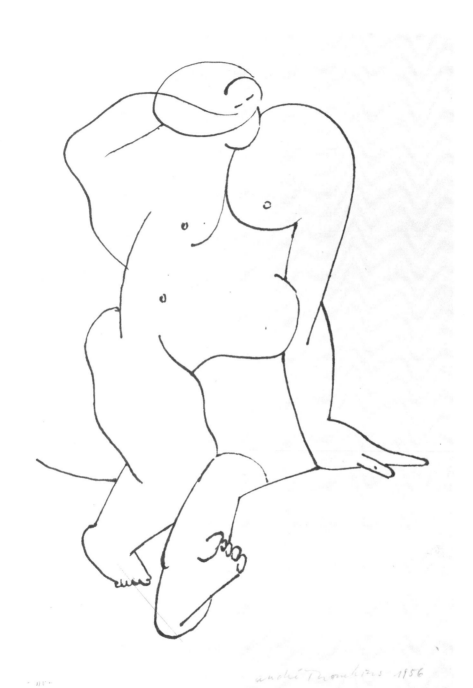

andré Tuomkens 1956

André Thomkins 1956

Nähe Füssli- André Thomkins 1956

61

- der Lächler -

André Thanlius 1956

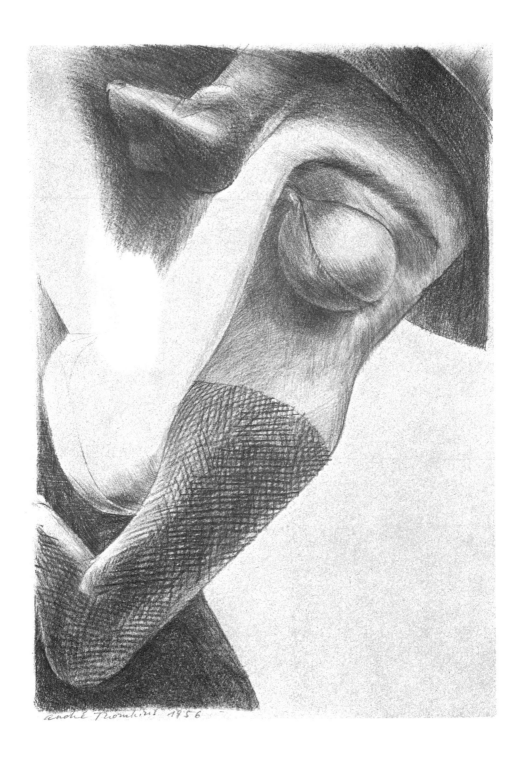

André Tromkins 1956

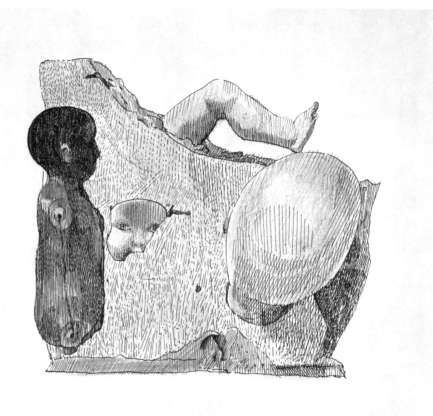

-schwarz-weiss-trümmer-

andl Thomkins 1956

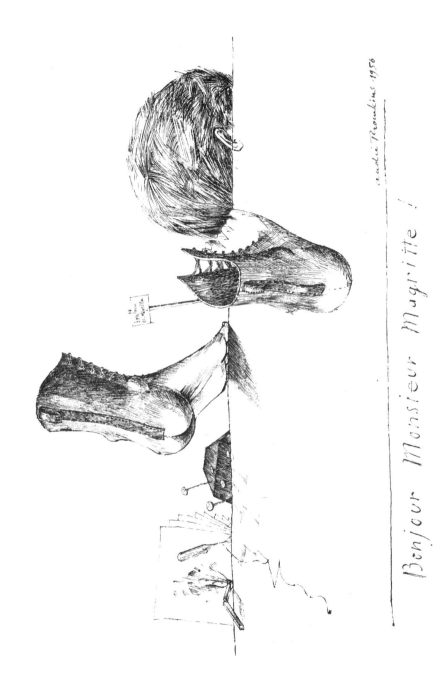

Bonjour Monsieur Magritte !

André Roualias · 1956

65

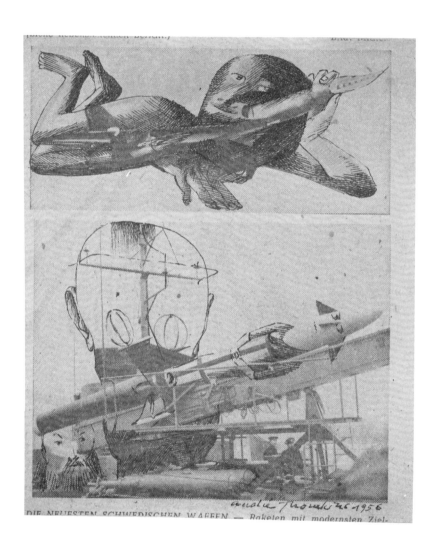

DIE NEUESTEN SCHWEDISCHEN WAFFEN — Raketen mit modernsten Ziel-

Die ersten deutschen Jeeps

Gleichsam als Weihnachtsgeschenk konnten Beamte des Verteidigungsministeriums am Samstag die ersten von einem deutschen Automobilwerk hergestellten Jeeps übernehmen. Die Fahrzeuge sind alle nach den Normen der NATO gebaut.

André Thomkins 1956

67

da das Schiff wegen des Streiks im New-Yorker Hafen nicht ausgeladen wurde. Dabei verlor der Junge 50 Pfund Gewicht. Jetzt wird Alfred in einem Krankenhaus bis zur Rückreise in die Heimat betreut.
up-Bild

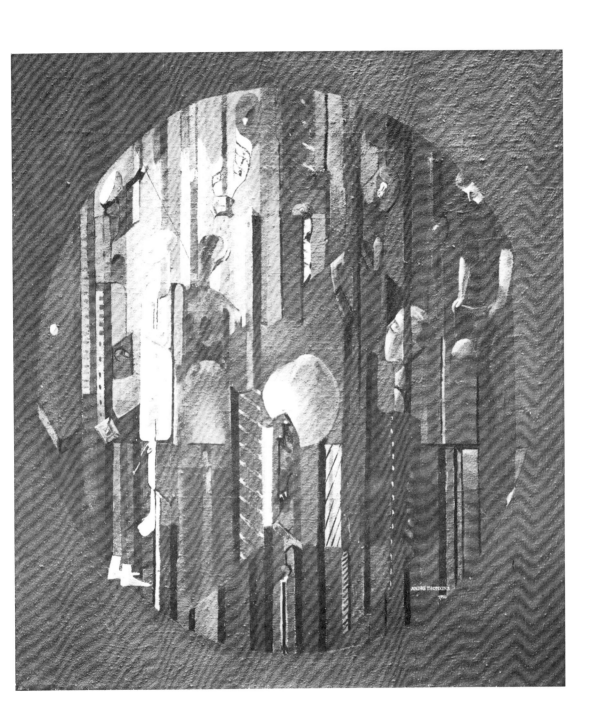

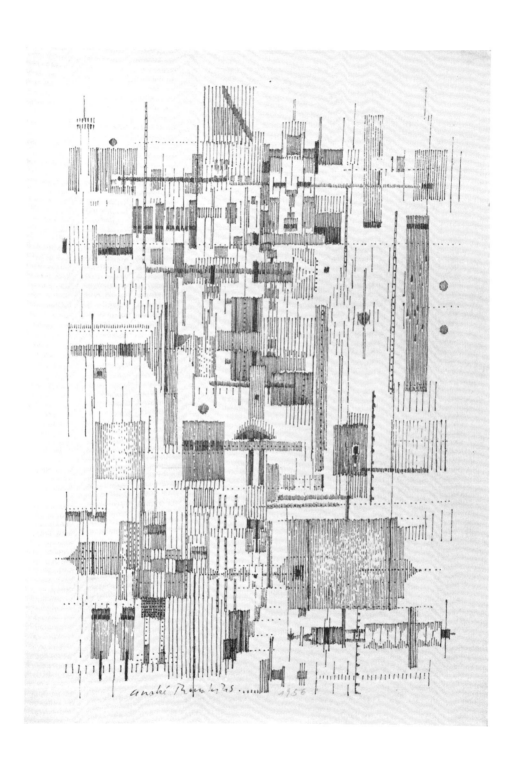

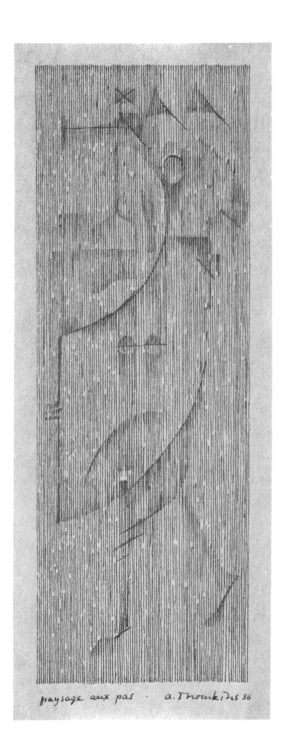

paysage aux pas · a. Tromkins 56

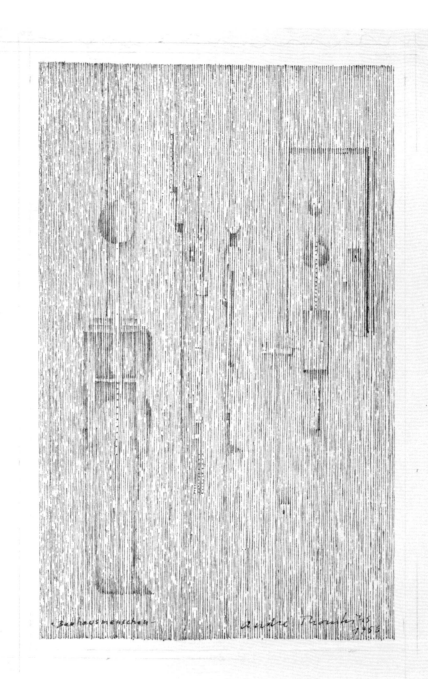

« Bauhausmenschen »   André Thomkins 1955

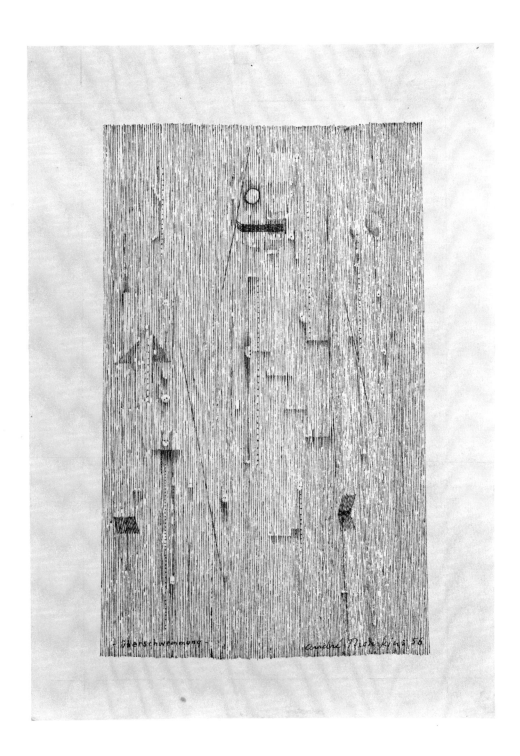

Überschwemmung   André Niederhäuser 56

'-phinuit-   andré Thombits 57

- anglers winkelzüge -

andré Thomkins 1957

Turmkochen, ein messopfer — andré Thomkins 1957

- Plastodont -

andré Tronkiens 1957

-bergreiter- andré Thomkins 1958

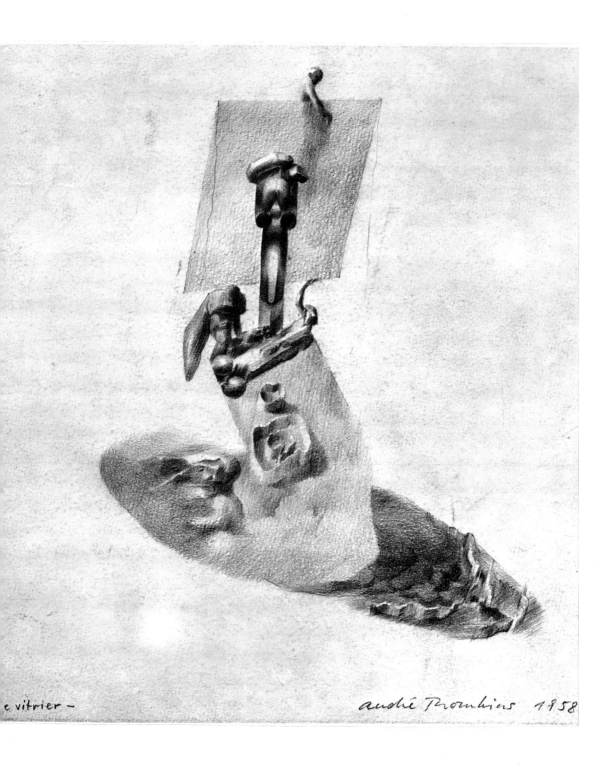

e vitrier —   andré Marchand 1958

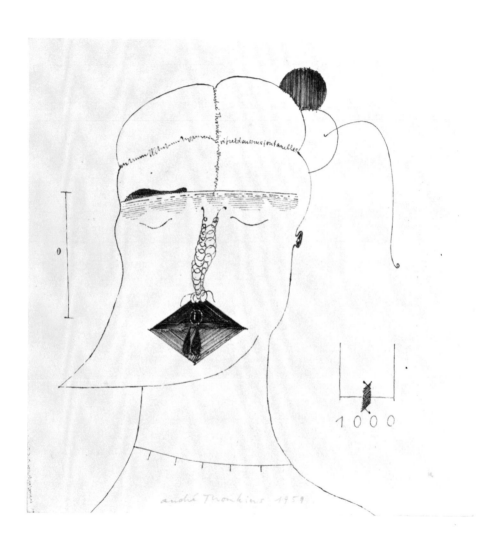

— aile aimant faire —   andré Thomkins 1958

—Thor—

andré Brouhns 1958

-zauber-   andré Thomkins 1958

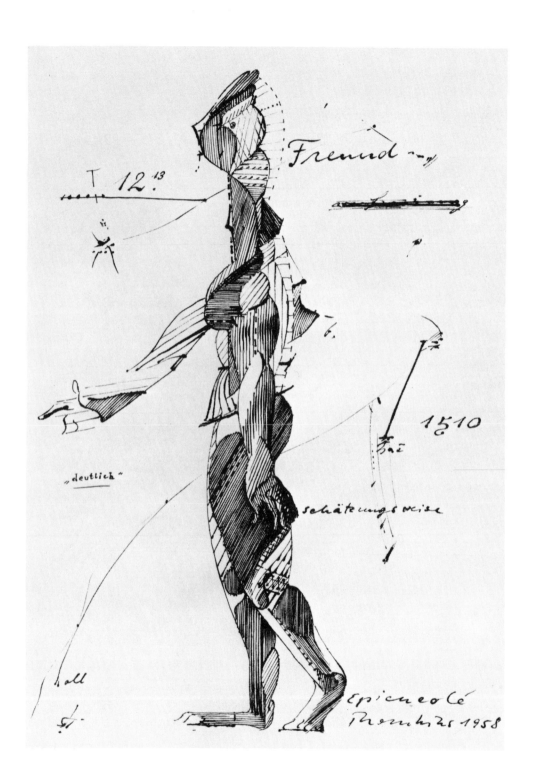

Freund

T 12.¹³

„deutlich"

1510

schätzungsweise

voll

Epicureté
Prometheus 1958

- unstilleben -

andré Thomkins 1958

André Thomkins 1959

- fingiertes fräulein -

andré Thomkins 1958

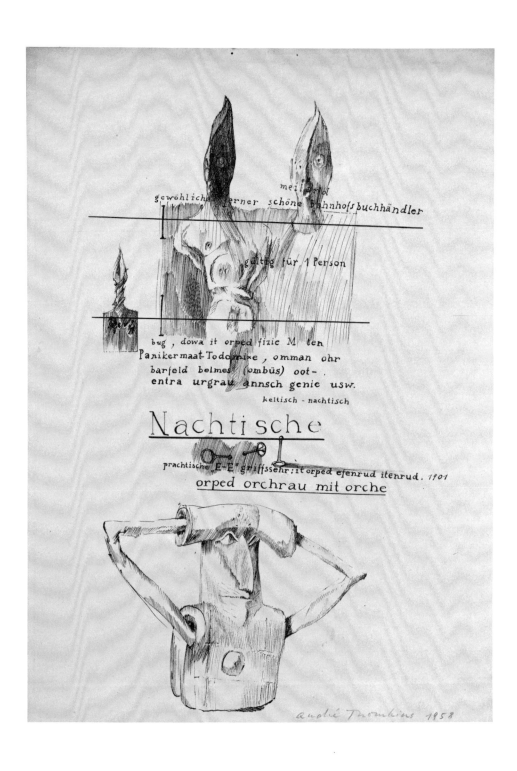

gewöhlich...erner schöne Bahnhofsbuchhändler

gültig für 1 Person

bug , dowa it orped fizie M ten
Panikermaat-Todomixe , omman ohr
barfeld belmes (ombüs) oot-
entra urgrau annsch genie usw.

keltisch - nachtisch

Nachtische

prachtische E-E griffssehr:it orped efenrud itenrud. 1901
orped orchrau mit orche

andré Thomkins 1958

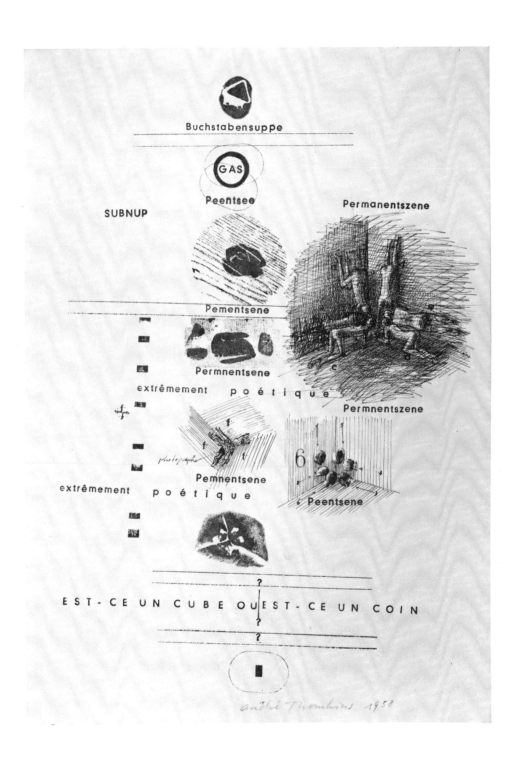

Buchstabensuppe

GAS

Peentsee

SUBNUP

Permanentszene

Pementsene

Permnentsene

extrêmement   poétique

Permnentszene

extrêmement   poétique

Pemnentsene

Peentsene

EST-CE UN CUBE OU EST-CE UN COIN

?
?
?

andré Thomkins 1958

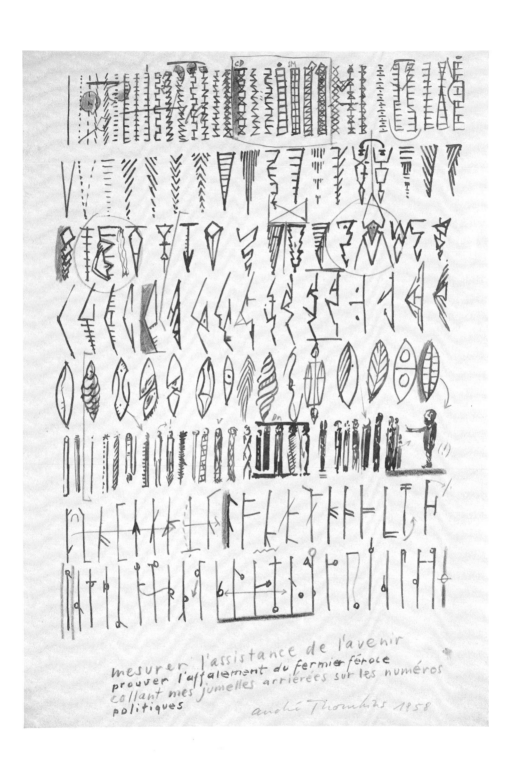

mesurer l'assistance de l'avenir
prouver l'affalement du fermier féroce
collant mes jumelles arriérées sur les numéros
politiques

andré Thomkins 1958

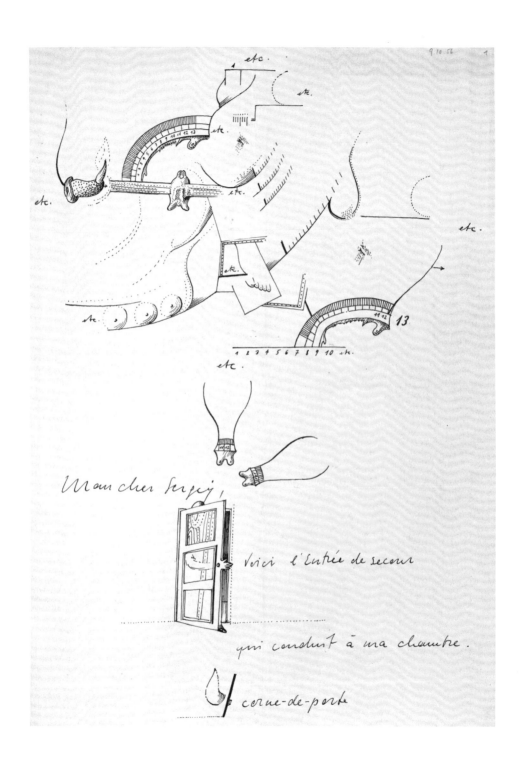

etc.

etc.

etc.

etc.

etc.

etc.

etc.

etc.

13

1 2 3 4 5 6 7 8 9 10 etc.

etc.

Mon cher Sergig,

Voici l'Entrée de secour

qui conduit à ma chambre.

corne-de-porte

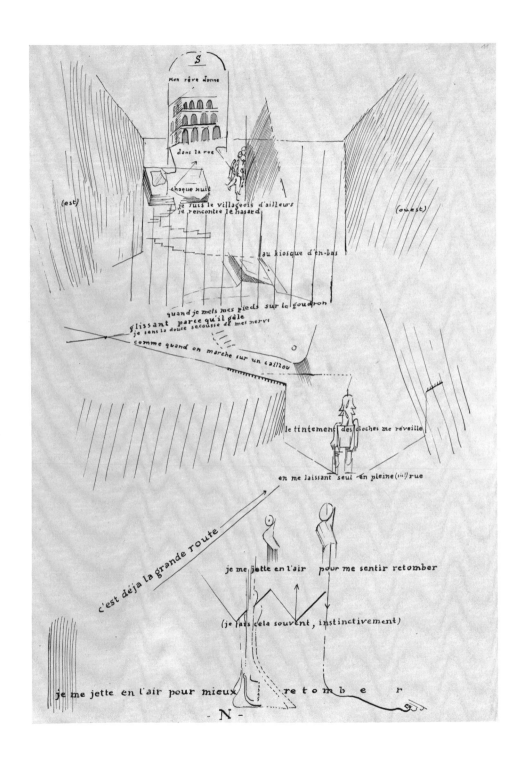

S

Mon rêve donne

dans la rue

chaque nuit

je suis le villageois d'ailleurs
je rencontre le hasard

(est)   (ouest)

au kiosque d'en-bas

quand je mets mes pieds sur le goudron
glissant parce qu'il gèle
je sens la douce secousse de mes nerfs

comme quand on marche sur un caillou

le tintement des cloches me réveille

en me laissant seul en pleine (sale) rue

c'est déjà la grande route

je me jette en l'air   pour me sentir retomber

(je fais cela souvent, instinctivement)

je me jette en l'air pour mieux   r e t o m b e r   r

- N -

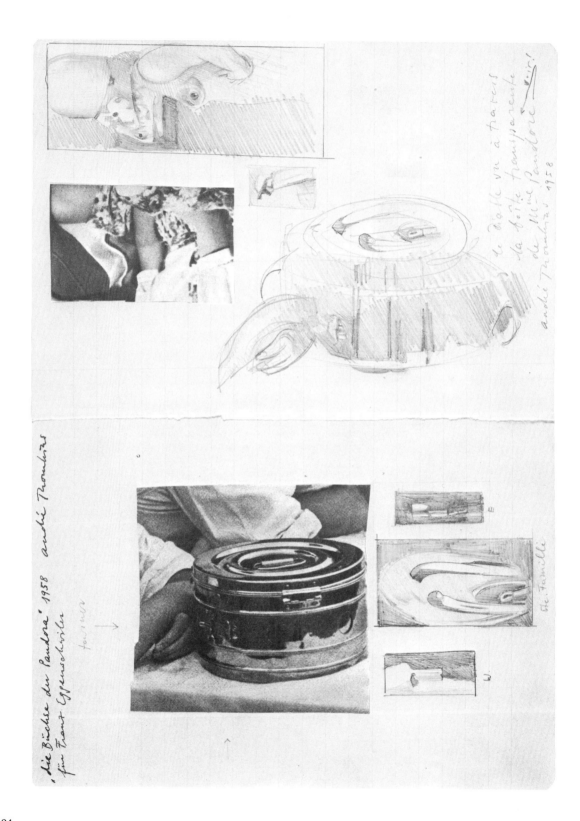

la Boîte vu à travers
la boîte transparente
de Mlle Pandore oui!

andré Thomkins 1958

"die Büchse der Pandora" 1958 andré Thomkins
für Franz Eggenschwiler

94

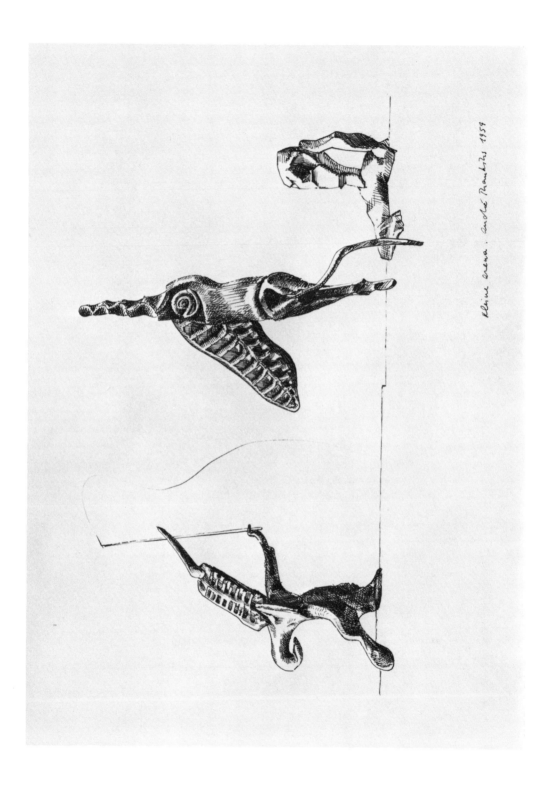

Kleine Szene · André Ramseyer 1959

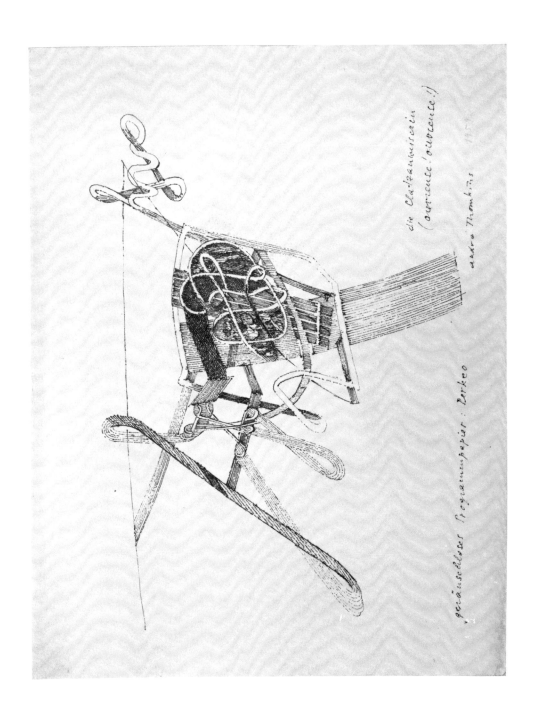

die Glatzhauserein
(oreille! oreille!)
extra Tomhirs 1957

gezäuseltes Programmpapier: Berleo

Blatt 32

Perkeo Lösch

weiß, etwa 275 g/qm

Nr. 66275   44,5/57,2 cm   etwa 70 kg

- fünf Fenster, eine Feder -

André Thomkins 1959

66275

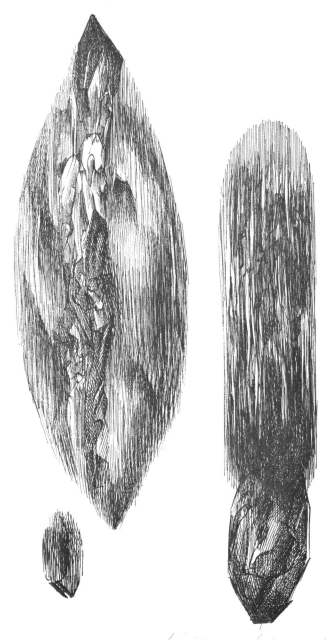

. zeitzeichen .   andré prünhires 1939

- spindelturm -   andré ?urnhius 1959

100

andré Thomkins 1959

(entweder mit eine—m—in berührung kommen, oder)

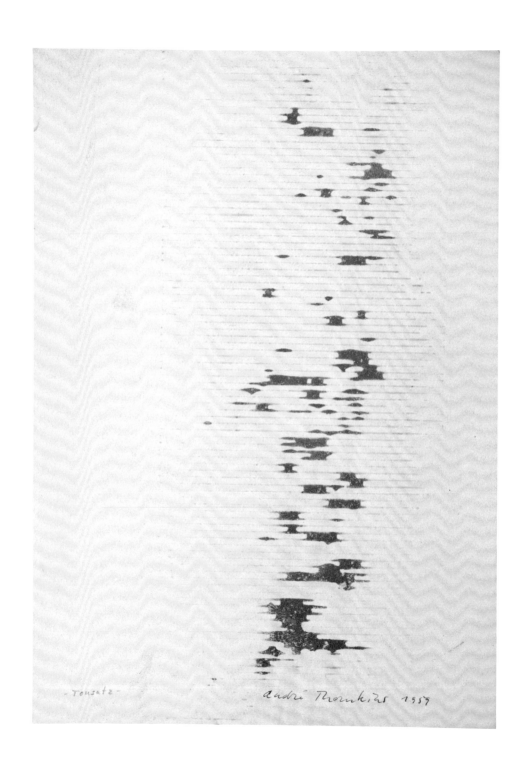

-Tonsatz-

André Thomkins 1959

- man agua -   d. Thiochies 1959

— le dictateur —   andré Thomkins 59

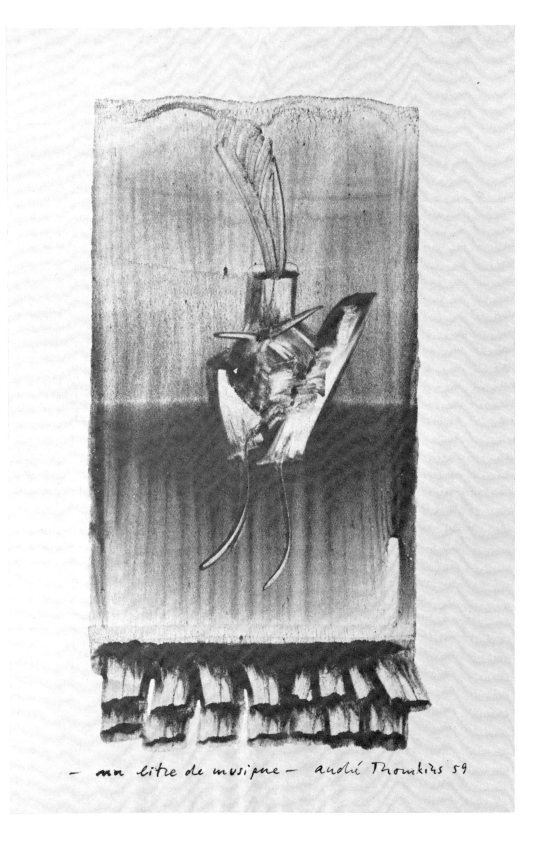

— un litre de musique — andré Thomkins 59

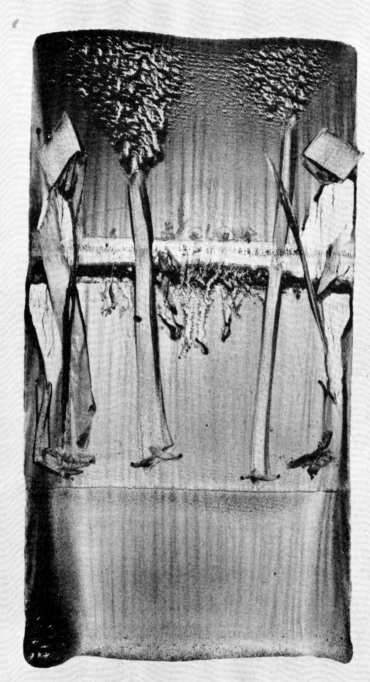

— die Wächter der Fatamorgana —   e.T. 1960

– Labyr –   André Thomkins   1960

- céphalopode -

andré Thomkins · 1961

- buddha -

andré Thomkins 1961

- der Traum vom Bodenlesen -

carola Thunders 1961

111

portrait
Scholz-Vollinghausen

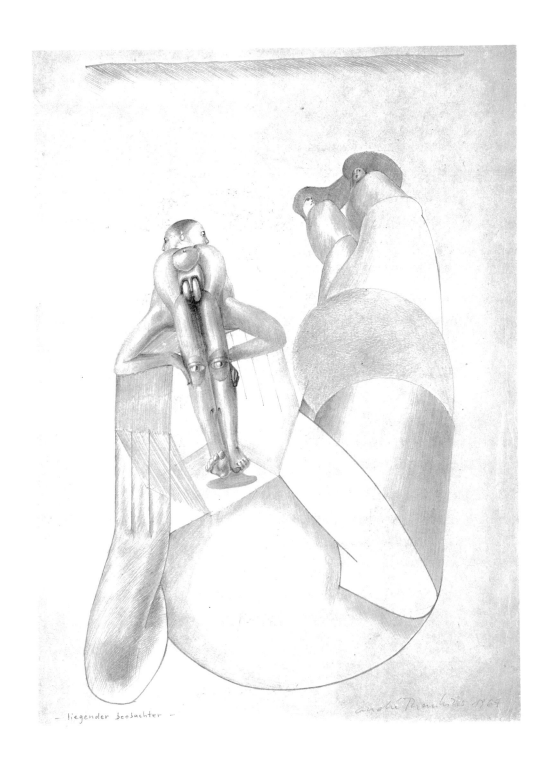

– liegender Beobachter –

Anatol Praub... 1969

André Thomkins 1964

– rechnen mit mal–durch–und–weg –

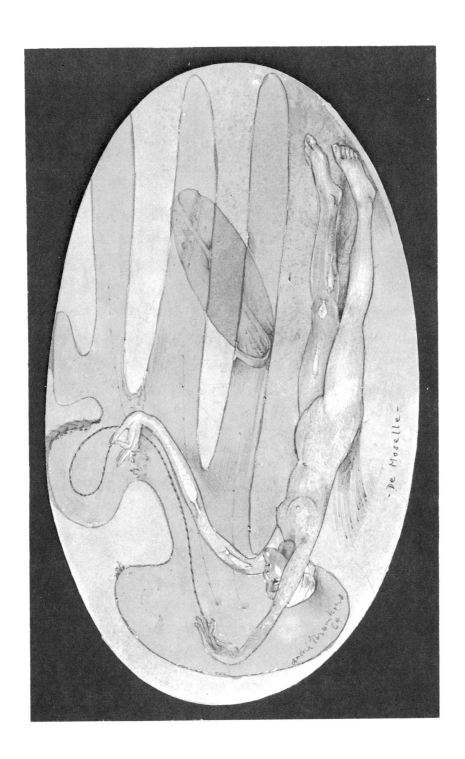

- De Moselle -

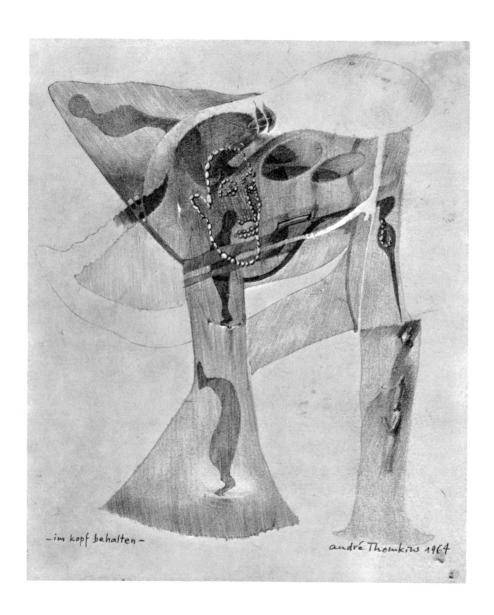

-im kopf behalten-

andré Thomkins 1964

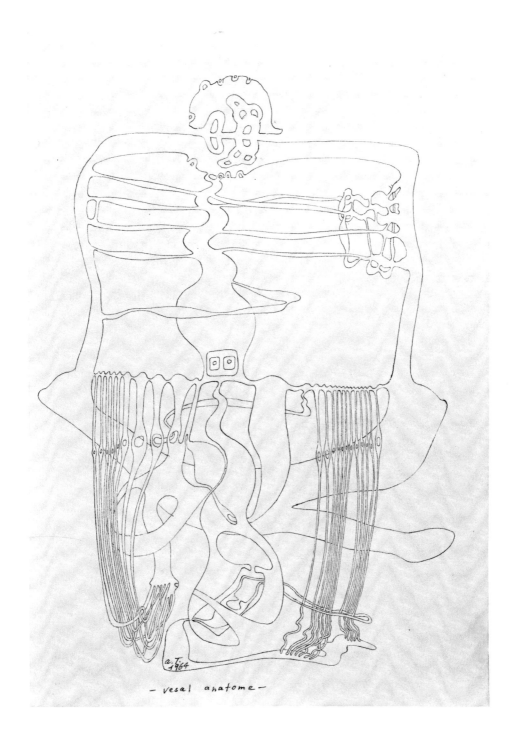

— vesal anatome —

andré Thomkins 1964   - Die Dialektik -

\- menschenmöglich -   andré Thomkins 1964

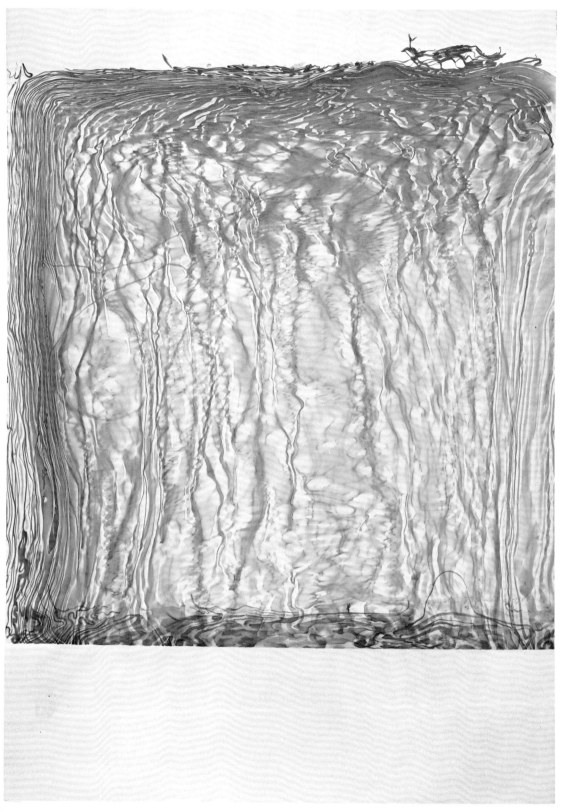

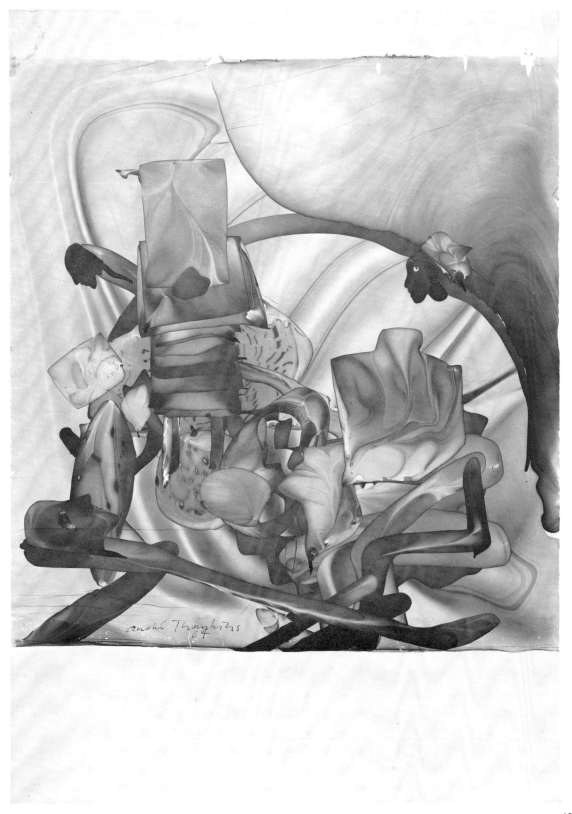

- Redon dance -

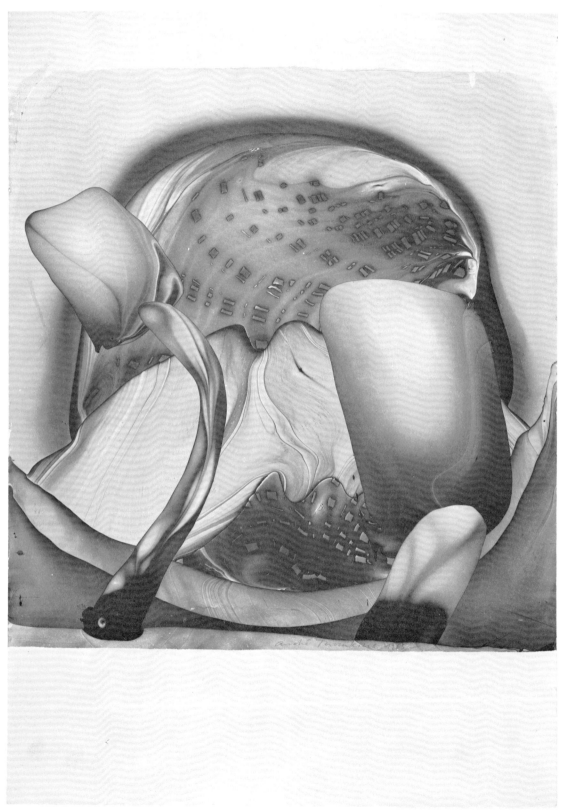

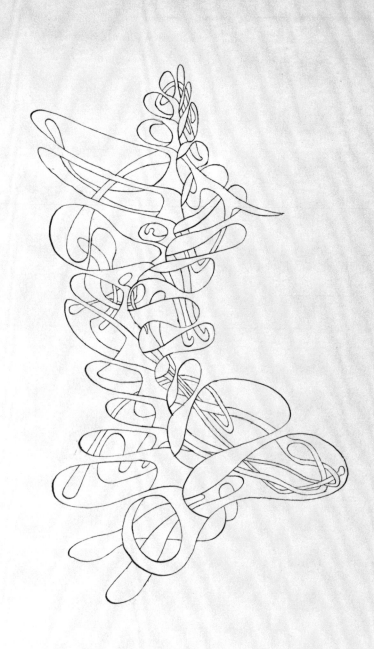

— endlos —

andré Thomkins 1965

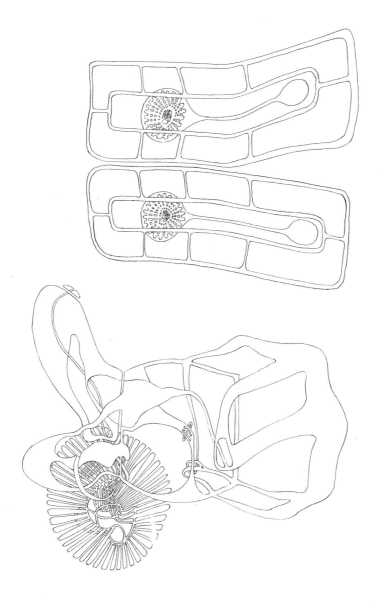

- Handlesen -

André Thomkins
1900

für Hand-& Fusssohin

La France et le Maroc et leur victime
Mhedi Ben Barka
(portolan a l'honneur d'Opicinus de Canistris)

andré Thomkins 1966

-Volkswagenprofil-

terra in orbis,
la méditerranée en tête

andré Thomkins
1966

-persönliche habe—

andré Thomkins
1966

andré Thomkins 1966

– antrop –

135

maison féité

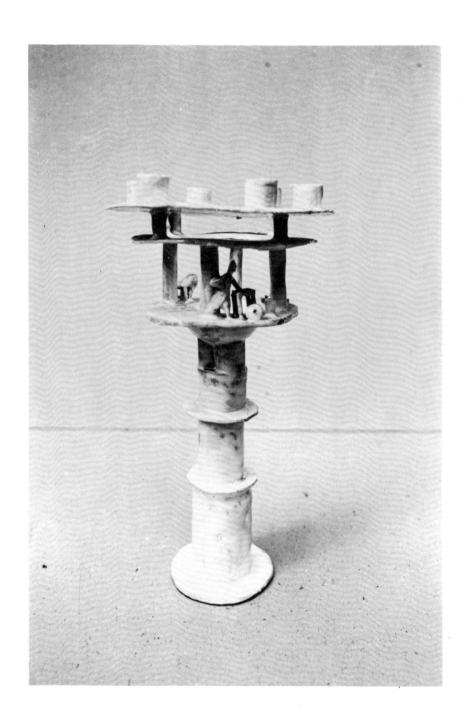

base nein – nase bein   A.T. 1966

140

ananatomie-   andré Rosenbiers 1967

–augohrmund–

andré Thomkins 1967

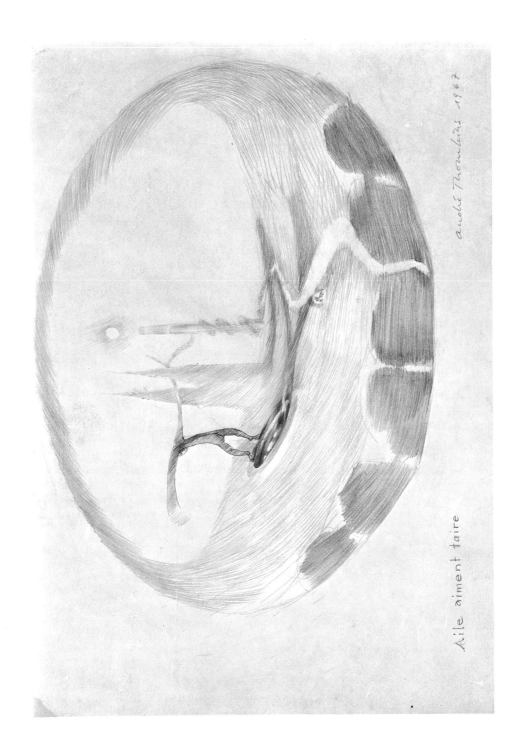

Arold Tremlers 1962

Aile aiment faire

143

- Kölner Embleme -   André Thoenkins 1967

144

- mit Diener aus Wien -

André Thomkins 1967

146

objet d'art à ne pas faire, peut-être : moulage en polyester
d'une bouteille et d'une assiette.

andré Thomkins 1962

147

» hurt heil, flieht heil, flieht heil, flieht ruh. « a.t.

» NEE, DIE IDEEN « a.t.

»→ TIMES EMIT ← a.t.

et il a su à ça:causalité a.t.

Rue La Valeur a.t.

» reflexelfer « a.t.

nie reime, da kann akademie rein a.t.

eher stier ebnete die wege, weideten bereits rehe a.t.

149

```
P E R M A N E N T E R F O R M W E G
R A M M W E N N P F O R T E R E G E
O P F E R W E R T M E N G E N A R M
G E R N O P F E R T A M M E N W E R
R E F O R M W E G P E R M A N E N T
A M O R F P E R M E N G E N W E R T
M E N G E W A R M E R T R O P F E N
M E N G E R N A P F W O R T M E E R
E R W O G E R N T E N M A M P F E R
E N O R M E R W E R T E M P F A N G
N E G E R O P F E R R A M M T W E N
T R O P F W E M M E E R G E R A N N
W A R E P E R M E N G E N F O R M T
E M P O R W E R F T G E R M A N E N
R E N N O P F E R R A M M T E W E G
F O R M P E R W A R T E M E N G E N
E P E N F O R M R E G N E T W A R M
N A R R T W E G F E R N E M P O E M
```

oTTo

andré Thomkins 1968

151

— cases communiquantes —   andré Thomkins 1968

– menschennetz –

andré Thombius 1968

153

–ist etwa etwas wie etwie etwa etwas wie etui ? andré thomkins 1968

eine Knabenpsychose nach georg fredrich —

Anolé Thomkins   1968

für David Sperry
zu seiner magie als noir, und als
Portrait vom Objekt 8

André Thomkins 1968

》 lies, magie zeig am seil! 《

auktion im Westphälischen   andré Thomkins 1968

'la belle poubelle'
für den mülleimer
Daniel Spoerri

andré
Thomkins
1969

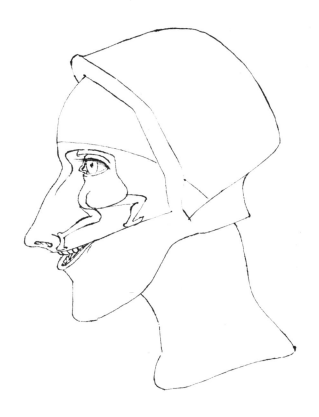

– Beinbeinhalten –   andré Thomkins 1969

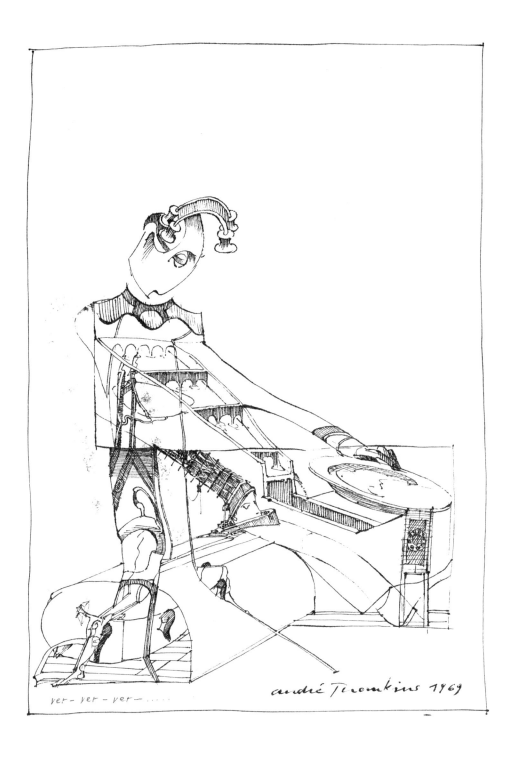

ver - ver - ver - .....

andré Thomkins 1969

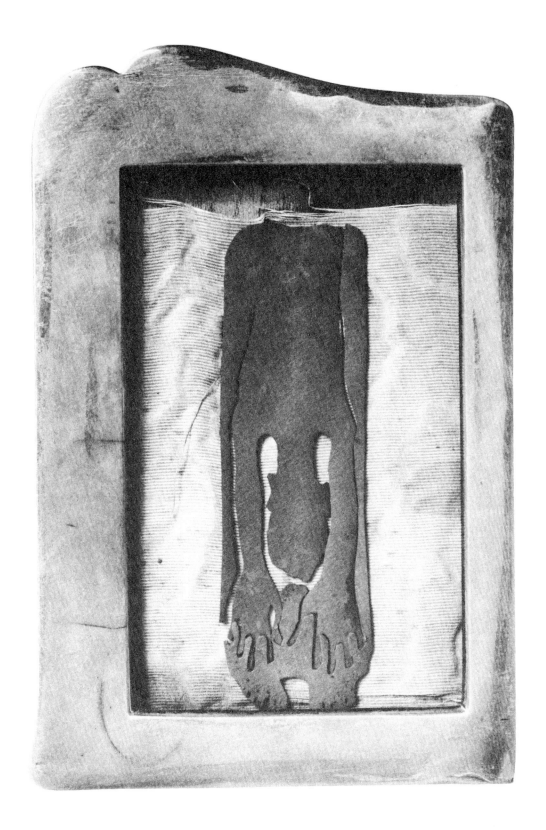

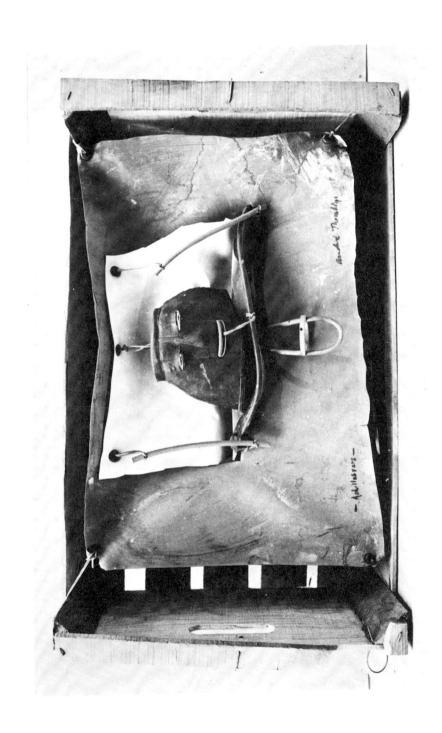

– le garde ne regarde pas ! –

André Thomkins 1969

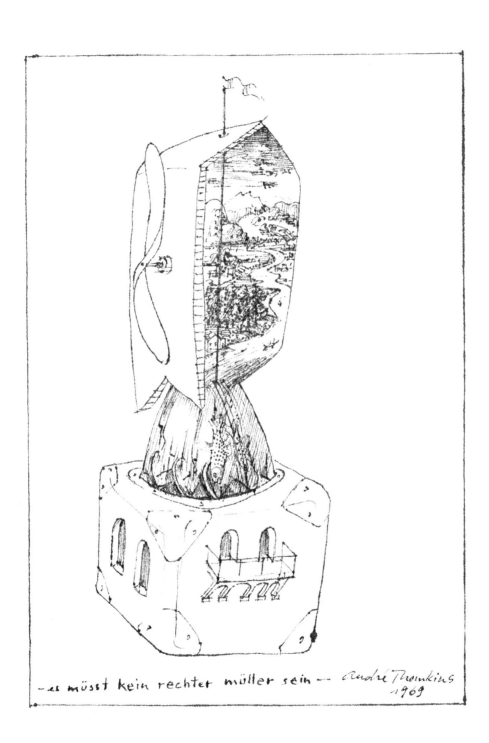

— es müsst kein rechter müller sein — André Thomkins
1969

166

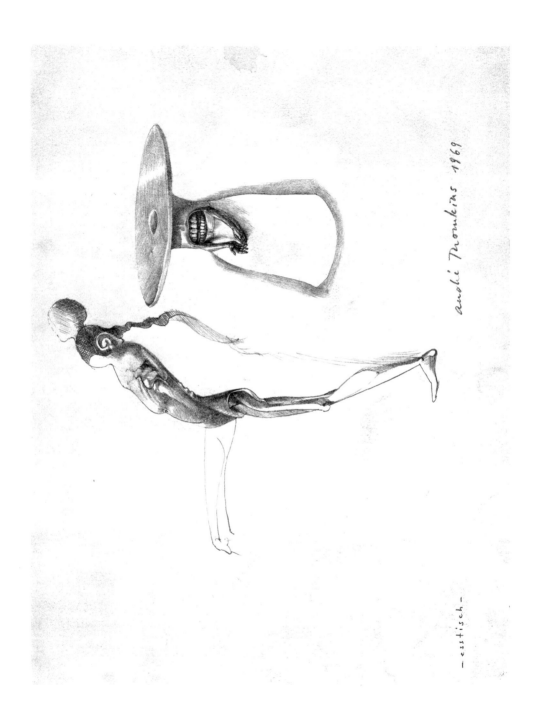

araoli Tronkias 1969

– esstisch –

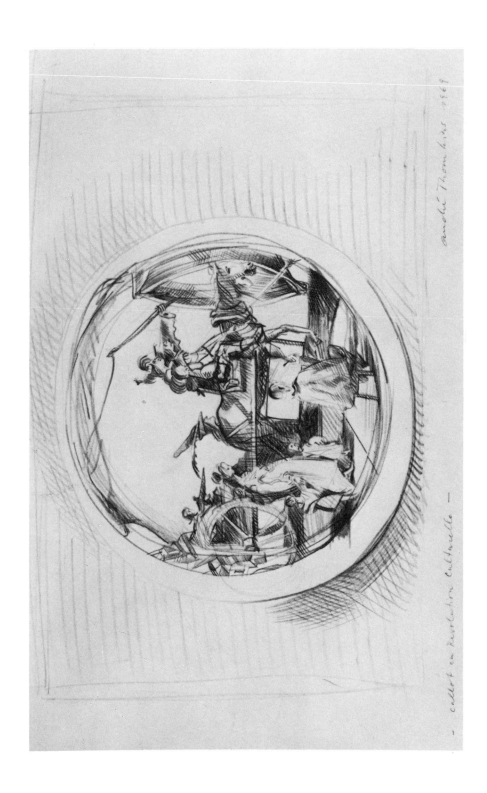

m. Callot

andré Trombière 1970

Füssli

andré Thomkins 1970

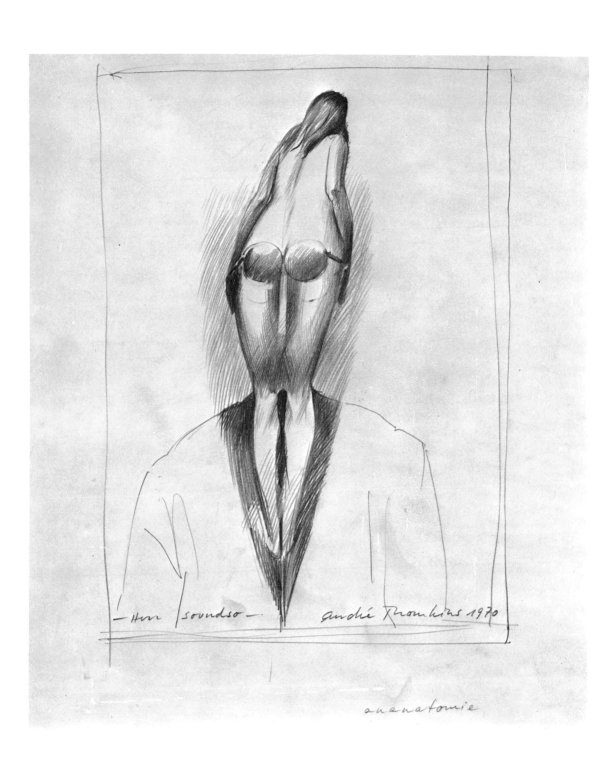

— Herr Soundso —   André Thomkins 1970

ananatomie

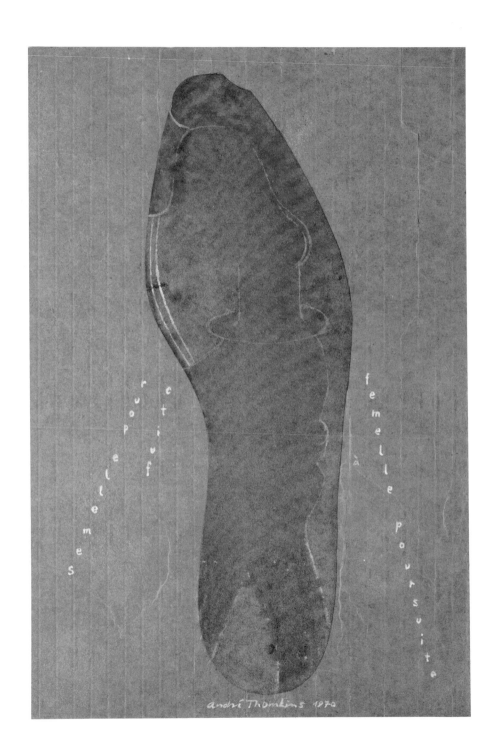

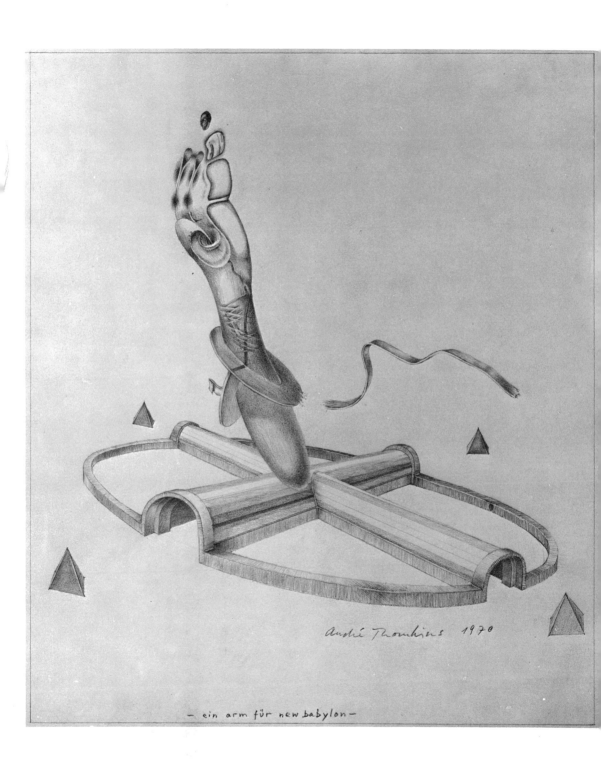

— ein arm für new babylon —

»nie besang nase sein«   andré Thomkins 1970

—Feldermädchen— André Thomkins 1950

für Franz Eggenschwiler – Drei flandrische Bauern –   André Thomkins 1970

177

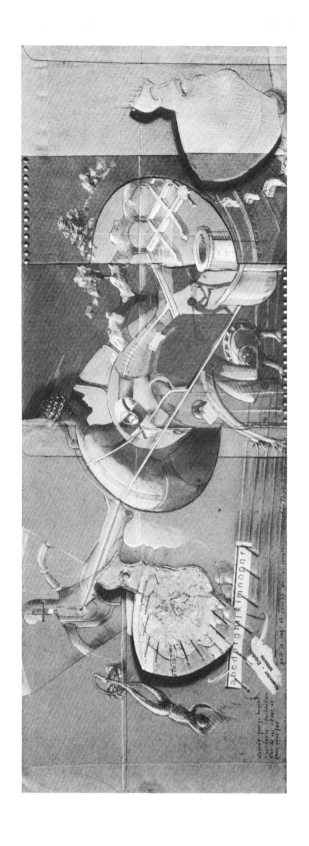

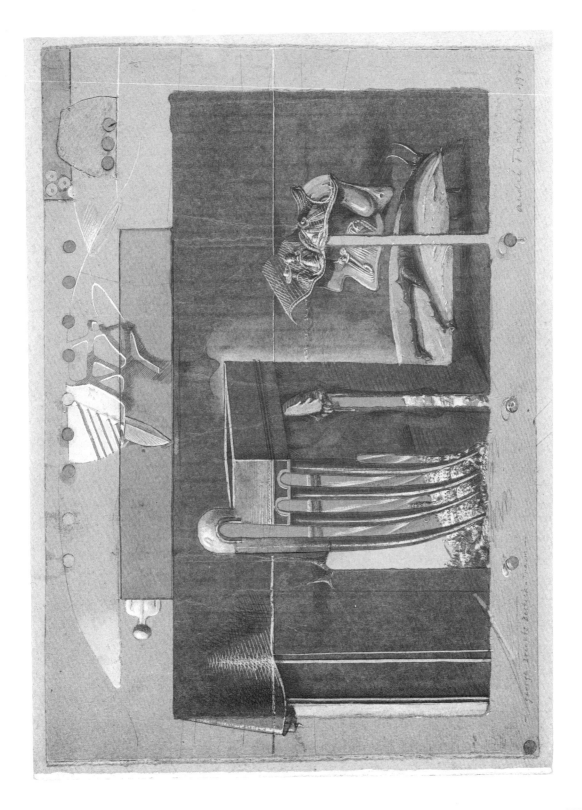

179

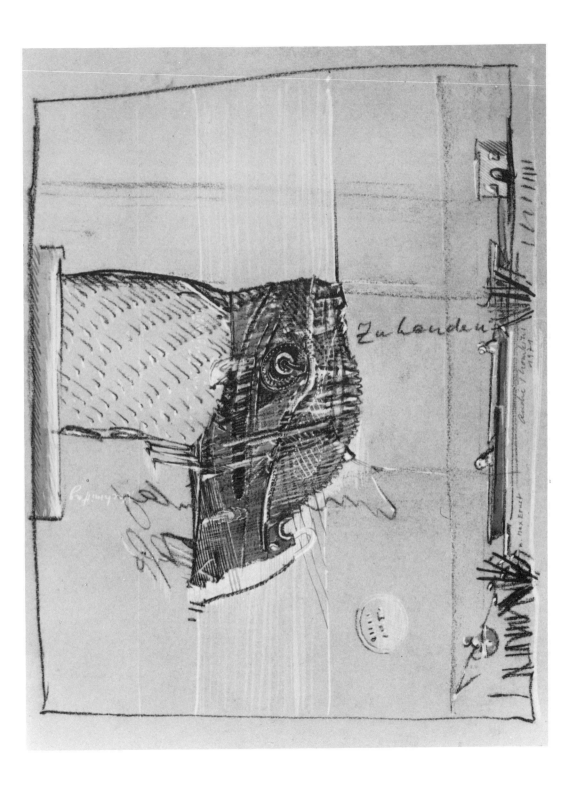

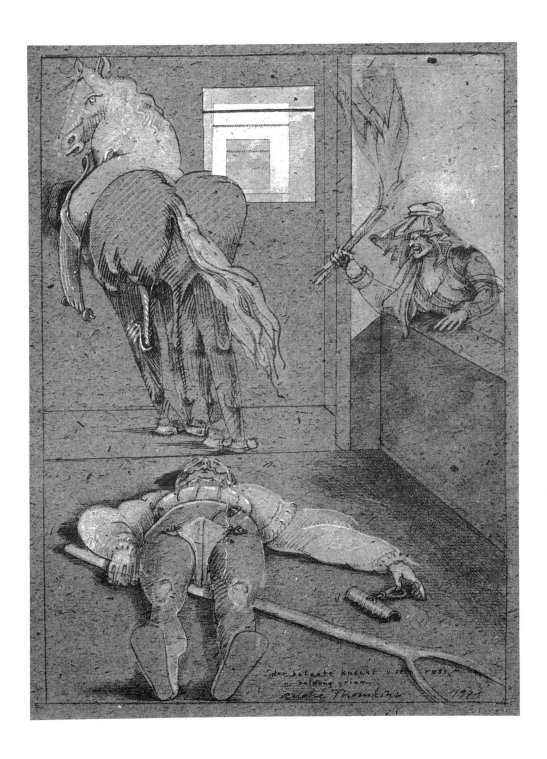

der behexte knecht u. sein ross,
n. baldung griem
André Thomkins   1971

n. Füssli   andré Thomkins 1971

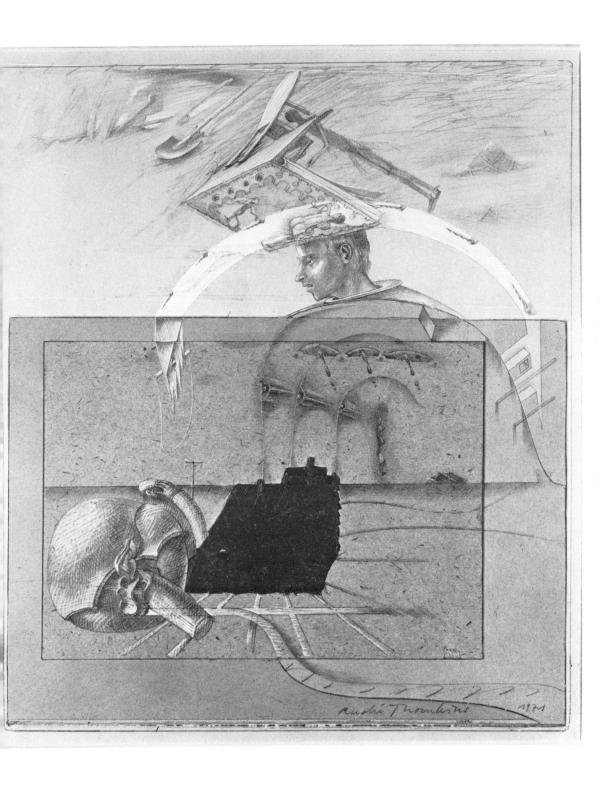

- josef -　　　　　　　　　　　　andré Thankins 1971

- waterwabe -

187

189

190

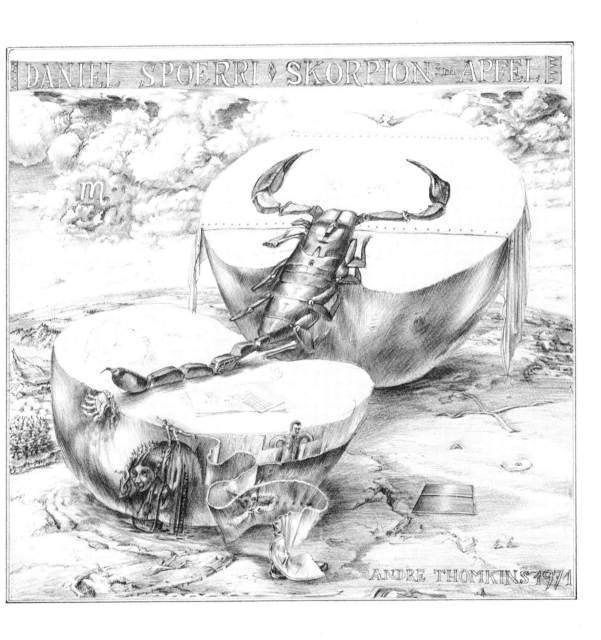

DANIEL SPOERRI · SKORPION im APFEL

ANDRE THOMKINS 1971

– aus einem grabmal in Worms –

andré Thomkins 1971

.. - Höhle bei Amalfi - andré Thomkins
1971

Raretal am Hasliberg

Gemalt Demelius 1922

194

Kreta, südküste *Anostt Trombus* *1992*

- schiff bruch - attentat -

andré Thomkins 1972

-kein türmen ohne landen-   andré Thomkins 1972

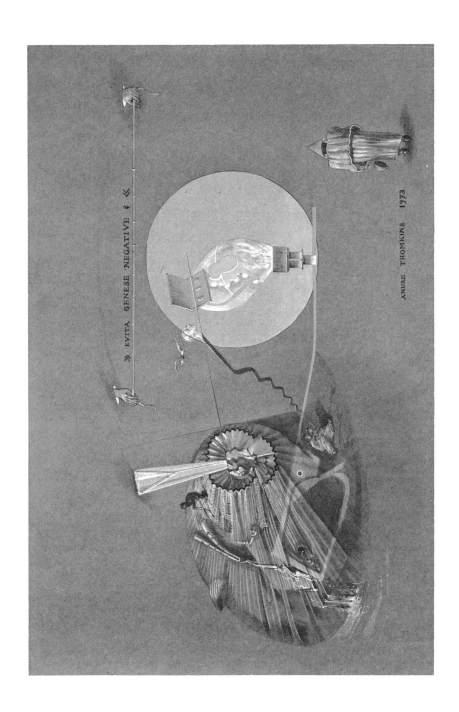

Felshöhle auf Kastai   andré Twombius 1973

202

Franz vor dem Plastic-Gespenst im vergifterten Weiher
bei Kevelaer   g. T.
73

Zimmer in Essen

a.Thomkins
1973

die "Überstunden" des Barbiers   André Thomkins 1974

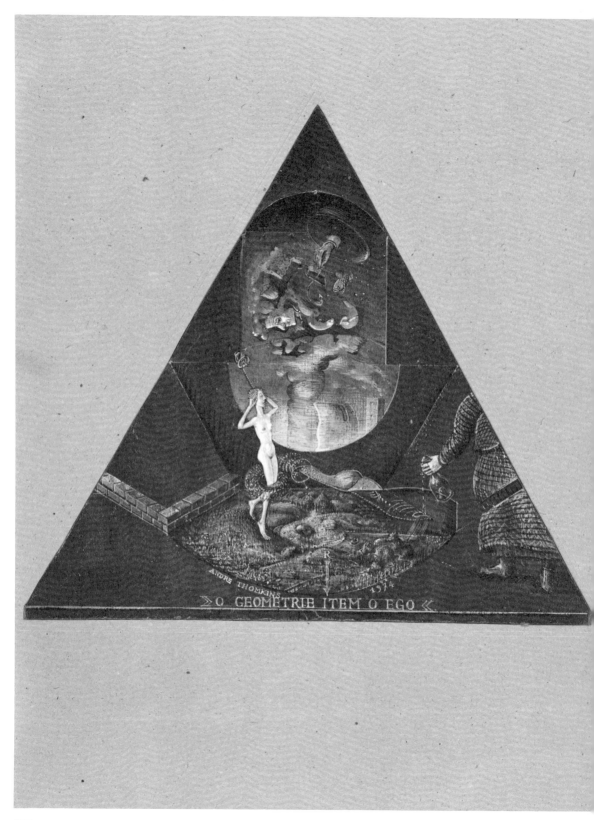

SLUIS

THOMKINS 1974

207

a.Thomkins 1974

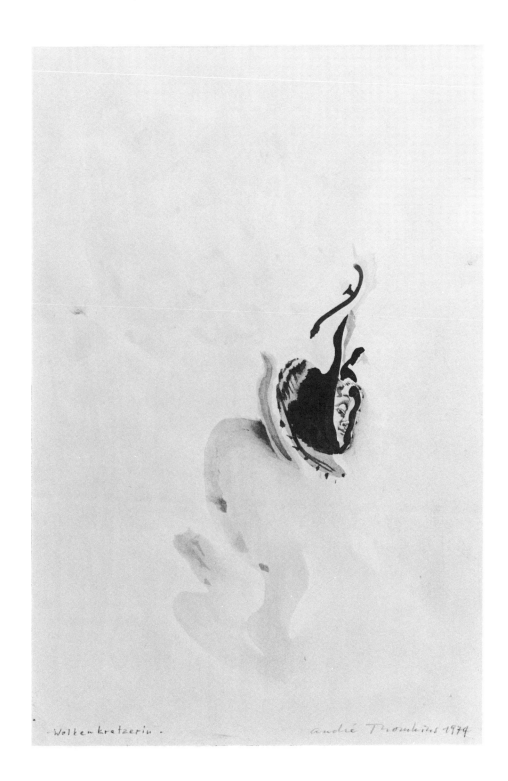

- Wolkenkratzerin -

andré Thomkins 1974

- Kinderspiel -

andré Thomkins 1974

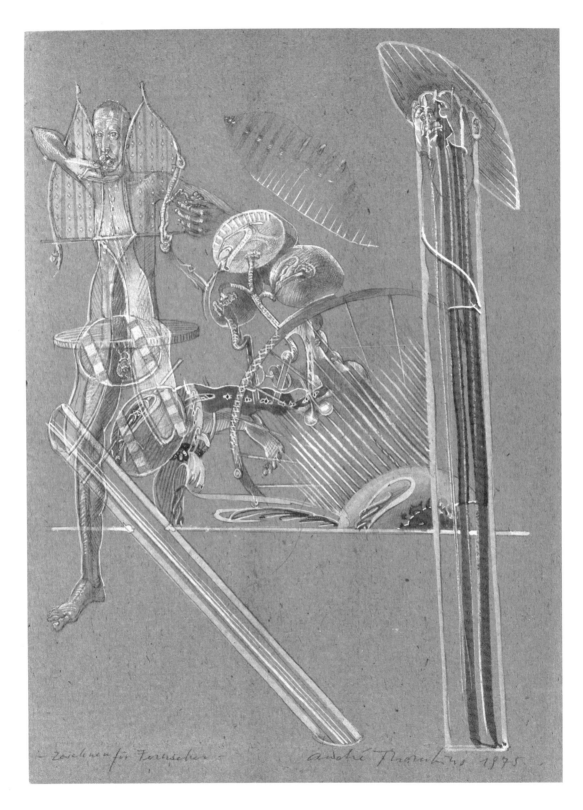

Zeichnen für Fortschte   André Thomkins 1975

-Zelebrieren + Praxis des Sammelns-

Dissipation des Passions d'ici —

André Thomkins 1975

DISSIPATION DENS PASSE D'ICI

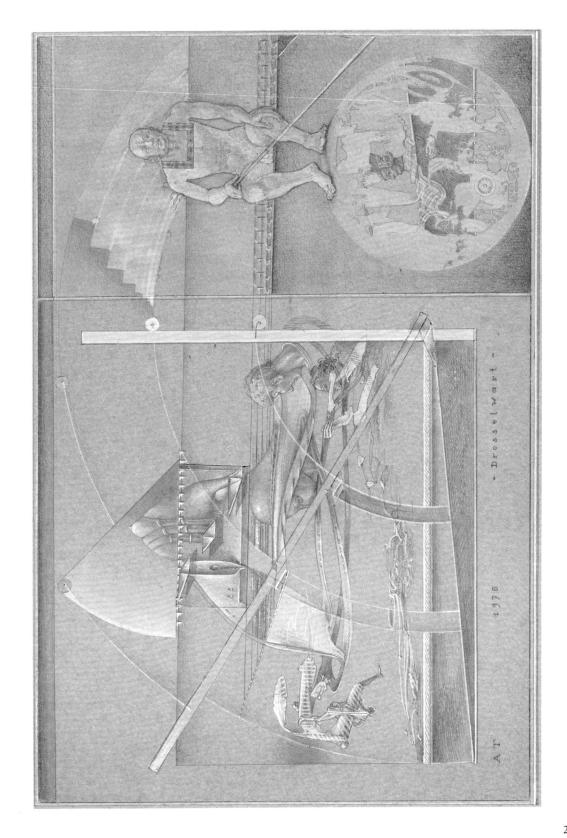

- Drosselwart -

A T   1975

215

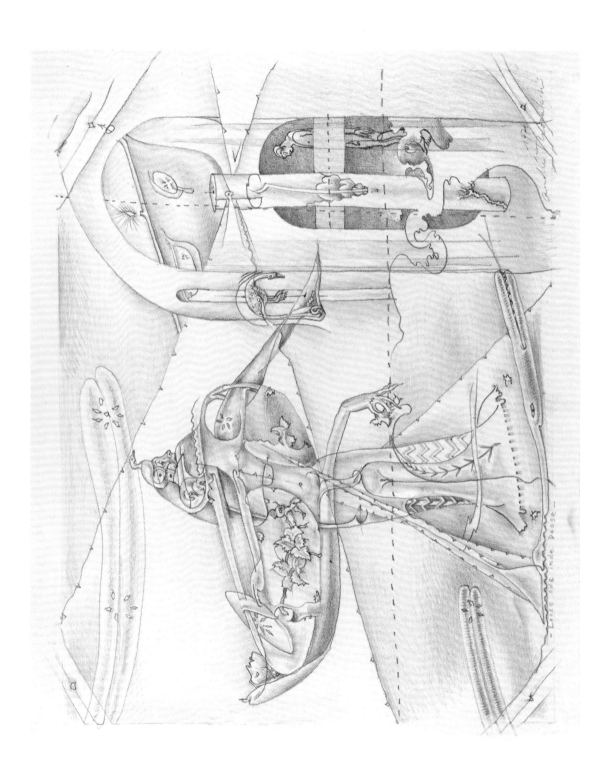

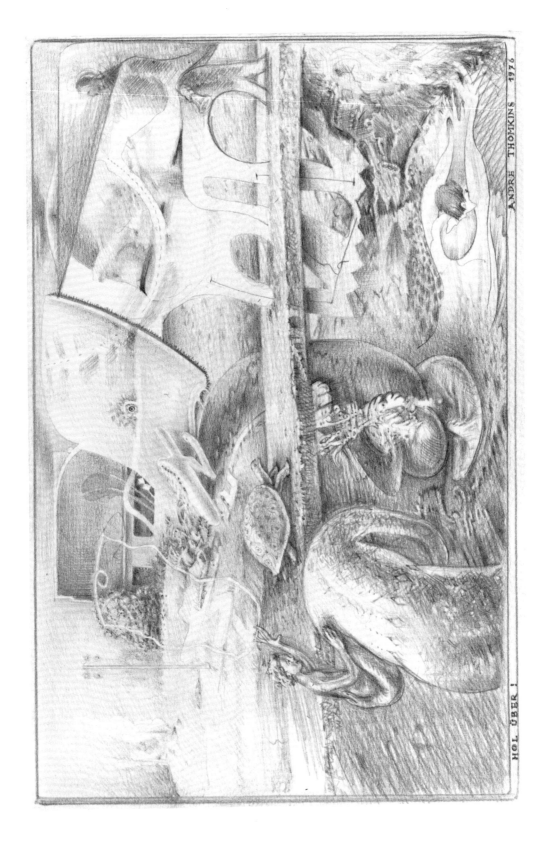

HOL ÜBER!

ANDRÉ THOMKINS 1976

217

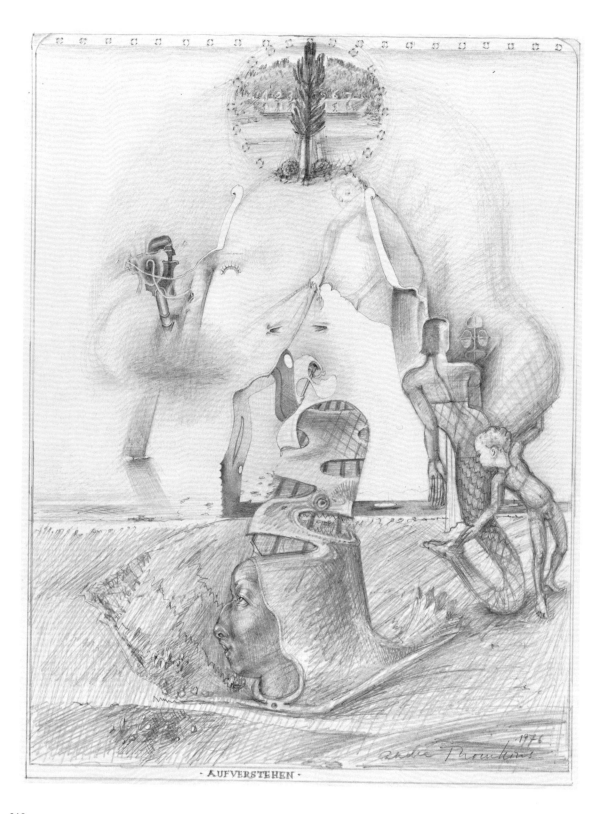

- AUFVERSTEHEN -

1976

andré Thomkins

- sos tenuto - André Thomkins 1977

- Pittura Metafisica -   andré Thomkins 1977

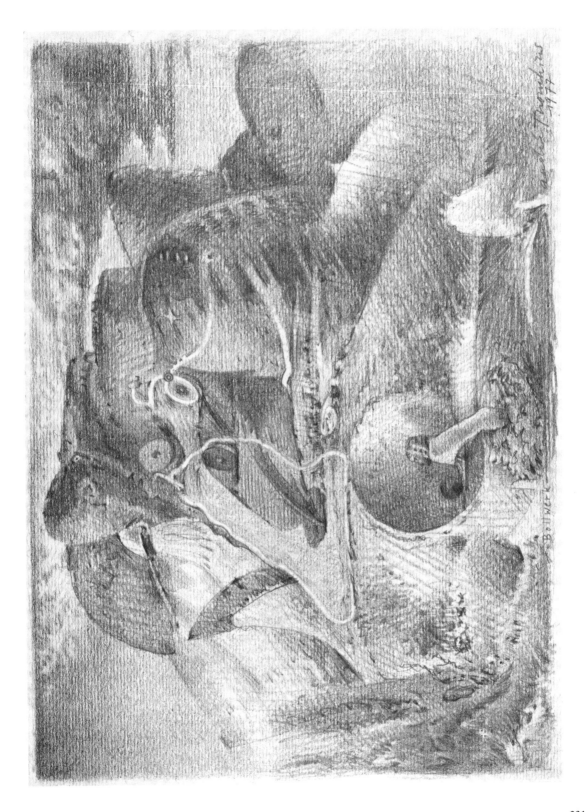

Bollwerk

221

DAPHNIS

- aesculap -   André Thomkins 1977

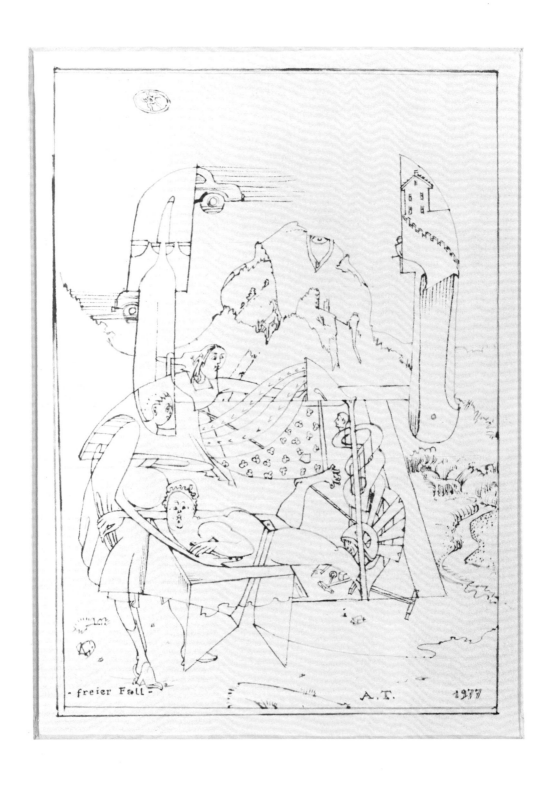

- freier Fall -   A.T.   1977

INSPIRATION AND METHOD

Karl Gerstner on the work of André Thomkins

Method in inspiration? Surely a paradox! Yet the question is worth pursuing particularly in the case of an artist from whom one would least expect an answer: André Thomkins, whose work consists of an overflowing stream of sketches — for pictures which he will probably never paint. Which is just what his teacher Max von Moos suspected.

It is a known fact: that Schiller used to keep in his desk drawer a rotten apple the smell of which used to inspire him when he was stumped for further matter to write. Less well-known is the fact: that Serge Golovin has unmasked this apple as a thorn apple — Datura stramonium — which, instead of going mushy and rotten, becomes dry and wizened; and by nibbling the peel one gets high. An alternative is to make a decoction of the peel and breathe in the vapour — which has helped many a witch onto her broomstick.

It is a known fact: that Hegel regularly had recourse to snuff. It is a less well-known fact, as more recent Hegel research has established, that in those days snuff was mixed with Cannabis indica — or hashish. Heiner Höfner reports: "During a lecture he took snuff so violently that the scatterings on his desk were sufficient to refresh his listeners." Hegel must have been in a constant state of euphoria, which might be an explanation of his rapturously poetic language.

Baudelaire did more than simply take hash in the Club des Hachichiens. William Burroughs wrote — generations later — first under the influence of hard drugs and later under the influence of their withdrawal. Huxley tried mescalin. Dali dripped strong perfumes on his eyelids. Modigliani simply got drunk before he painted — and, Heaven only knows, he wasn't the only one: "Most Americans", wrote Norman Mailer, "find intellectual inspiration only under the influence of alcohol." And, Heaven only knows, not only the Americans.

The use of drugs is drastic, but there is method in it, like madness: van Gogh ate the oil paints with which he painted his pictures in order to achieve the unio mystica.

There are also more subtle methods: Dostoiewski needed the kick of gaming for high stakes to become active just as Robert Walser needed the tranquillity of long walks.

These are possible answers to the question: *how* inspiration can be invoked. To *what* an artist can be stimulated is another question.

Douanier Rousseau not only obtained vague inspiration from department store catalogues but simply copied what seemed to him to be useful. There is a famous picture by René Magritte from the year 1927 — "The Man with the Newspaper" —, which is a faithful copy of an anonymous xylograph from the year 1899.

Konrad Klapheck collects pictures of all the typewriters, calculators, machine tools and other machines he can get hold of in illustrated magazines, catalogues and technical works. He arranges them with the conscientiousness of a good book-keeper in suitably inscribed envelopes which provide him with an inexhaustible source of inspiration for future pictures. It may be supposed that one of these days he will paint a helicopter. This is a theme he has been collecting for long enough without yet having put it into paint.

Others do not nourish their inspiration from others but rather imbibe it from their own breast — the logical use of the bachelor machine! Like Marcel Proust, they live their lives a second time in their works.

Thus, in his "tram stop", which he showed at the last Biennale, Joseph Beuys worked over a key experience from his childhood. At a tram stop in Cleves he decided to become a sculptor — which, if one delves more deeply into Beuys, is not so bizarre as it might first appear.

228

Every time he came to this tram stop, where he often had to change trams, he saw an arrangement of obsolete culverins and bombards which the governor of Cleves, Moritz von Nassau, had ordered to be placed there at the end of the 17th century. Moritz von Nassau, it should be explained, designed arrangements like the one at the tram stop in a grandiose style according to geometrical-mystical criteria. I can easily imagine how impressed the young Beuys was; how he, as he says today, came to see that out of materials one can make something which transfers meaning.

Looking at "tram stop" with this knowledge in mind, one discovers that it reconstructs Beuys's memory, as it were, materially and naturalistically on a scale of 1 : 1. One can see the actual tram rail, see that the barrel of an old cannon supplies the pedestal for what is sculpture in the classic sense of the word: a portrait bust which Beuys did shortly after his studies with Mataré.

In the case of the composer Dieter Schnebel something can be clearly observed which is only vaguely true of many others: that precisely those works which are markedly avantgardistic — such as "Maulwerke" — are nothing else but the, so to say, linear continuation of musical history (— typically, the critics say in such cases: this is really going too far . . .).

Conversely, but no less clearly, Marcel Duchamp was at pains to break with historical development.

Think yourself back to 1914 and try to imagine what would be the greatest possible contrast to everything that had previously rated as a work of art — and you come almost automatically to the "readymade": the most banal of everyday objects in contrast to the work of art whose criterion is exceptionality: the mass-produced hat-rack, the snow shovel, the typewriter cover in contrast to the solitary originality of the work of art.

In the "readymade" Marcel Duchamp simply declared the work of anti-art to be a work of art. In the "readymade réciproque" he retraced his steps and transmogrified the Mona Lisa into an ironing board. And in the "readymade anticipé" he did something which was to be of far-reaching significance for the next generations of artists: he made a method out of chance.

What always impressed me so much about Marcel Duchamp was the radicality of his method of thinking the unthinkable. This can also be seen in the fact that the virile Duchamp gave himself, of all things, the identity of a woman, the immortal Rose Sélavy, perhaps his most sensitive creation.

It may also happen that the method of inspiration is not only a means to an end but is also as important as the work itself. This is the case with Raymond Roussel, whose main works include "Comment j'ai écrit certains de mes livres" — a detailed account of the method which is to be read with the same astonishment and admiration as his other books.

There's no end to the subject, and before I get irretrievably lost, I will draw the conclusion: that there is no end to it because each artist has his own method or methods of finding inspiration. Indeed: one might even say that this is where his real gift and importance lie. This is the brainwork; the rest is craft, routine.

Now what are the methods which André Thomkins makes his very own?

It comes as no little surprise to realize that at least some of his methods are not only peculiarly his own but also extremely old. For instance: when he rearranges letters, makes anagrams — something he has been doing all his working life.

With this method, which cannot be more banal, he discovers words, concepts, which could not be more original. For instance, the "Denkharmonist" (thought harmonist) behind which are hidden the letters of his name André Thomkins. The letters of my own name Karl Gerstner he turned round to make "Streng Klarer" (the strict clear one).

André Thomkins derived the most incredible anagram from the title of my book "Programme entwerfen" (Designing Programmes). It contains eighteen letters out of which he made eighteen anagrams, i. e. an anagram squared. Thus "Programme entwerfen" became in this way "Enormer Wertempfang" (Enormous value reception), or "Permanenter Formweg" (Permanent form way), or "Form per Wartemengen" (Form through waiting quantities). The latter anagram in particular describes what the book is about in a way which is as succinct as it is surprising. Programming is simply that: to elicit specific forms from the totality of all existing forms — the waiting quantities that is.

The method of anagrams produces creations which would never have occurred to anyone otherwise, but which might occur to anyone to whom the method had occurred.

He does much the same thing with another equally old method: that of the palindrome. These are words and phrases which astonish one by being readable backwards and forwards. "Oh cet écho" (— please read again from right to left!). André Thomkins also found a name for a professional exponent of this method

— a "retroworter". Here again he becomes linguistically creative via method; or he opens up new dimensions in conventional language, which he speaks in various tongues.

On the "Rue La Valeur", Value Street, he, like Archimedes before him, comes upon his eureka: "Strategy! get Arts". In German, a certain scepticism is in place: "Reize vitaler Stiere bereits relative Zier" (The charms of vital bulls already a relative ornament).

Schopenhauer has gone down in history with only one palindrome "Ein Neger mit Gazelle zagt im Regen nie"; André Thomkins has so far produced several hundred. That is his yardstick, to find something new in methods that are old. Now and again he even finds new ones.

As in the case of the "Dogmat-Mot". This is a polyglot machine of words which are written the same way in different languages — German and French, French and English, English and German — but mean something different. The word "Donner" (thunder) is read in French as "donner" (give); the word Taste (key) is read by an Englishman as "Taste", and so forth. These simple double meanings give rise to implications which Thomkins fructifies many times over in the form of "mobile dogmas".

Considering the way he understands language, it is no coincidence that André Thomkins has a knowledge of literature which is built up on very unusual principles, not perhaps so much in regard to extent as to content. He is a walking anthology of everything that is out of the way — and this, too, I am inclined to regard as method. His knowledge, if not secret, is nevertheless mysterious; a power station where he can charge his batteries time and time again.

Given his philosophy that art consists in making something out of something, André Thomkins doesn't mind very much what he makes out of what. Without a passport he slips lightly over well-guarded frontiers; say, that between word and image.

Often his pictures proceed by the most direct route from the images already inherent in language. He takes a word as a word and shows a "Mutter" both as a "mother" and also as a "nut", which is another meaning of the same German word. I have a drawing entitled "knee psychosis". He read the word in Georg Grodeck, picked it up and, like an illustrator, gave it a credible representational form. If there is to be a "knee psychosis" — and after all, why not? — then I cannot visualize it in any other way than that in which André Thomkins portrays it.

To illustrate language means, in the last analysis, nothing else but to present the pictures it conveys. As a method of inspiration that provides material for several life's works. But not for André Thomkins.

Just as he uses language as a datum, as material, so he also lets materials themselves inspire pictures for him. To mark an occasion, he made for Ben Vautier postcard-size sculptures out of rubber bands — which started a mighty production of rubber sculptures. Everything industry makes out of rubber — from door-stops to inner tubes — André Thomkins combined to make objects beyond number.

For Daniel Spoerri's "Eat Art" André Thomkins made objects out of pasta and sugar. Imagine: constructions of spaghetti, macaroni, crescent noodles; of lump sugar, candy sugar, liquorice — again something no one else would think of unless he works towards his goal as methodically and uncompromisingly as André Thomkins. With the comestibles he does justice to the "Eat" in "Eat Art", and with the choice of pasta and sugar he does justice to the "Art" in "Eat Art": for these materials never go bad — an essential characteristic of a work of art.

There's another way in which André Thomkins may be said to come to art from material. For instance, when he declares an illustration out of the "Geographical Magazine" to be a permanent scene just as it is. Or when he takes illustrations from newspaper and magazines and alters them with a few strokes in such a way that they acquire one or more extra meanings in addition to their original meaning.

However, in these cases we already have intimations of another very specific method of André Thomkins, which is not so easily reproduced as the anagram or the palindrome. Here he practises a kind of vision from a lofty point of vantage, which he also uses in other methods.

For instance, in his repeat-of-pattern pictures, where the method consists in drawing on an empty surface a basic pattern which is, at the outset, utterly uninspired. As he goes on differentiating this basic pattern there arise — quite literally — figurations and figures under his hand. The whole — as it becomes denser and denser — ends in an apotheosis of anatomical components, of faces and bodies, of pictures of fauna and flora, real and imaginary, of landscapes, townscapes; all woven into the original network in a breath-taking mixture of every conceivable scale and perspective.

Thomkins calls this method of filling in fields the formulary method. It is constructive in distinction to the fundamentally different baroque method which consists in making free brush-strokes, usually light-coloured patches, on the paper at random. As the work proceeds, he "reads" these patches in a representational fashion. Just as in the formulary method, he constantly deciphers in them new figurations and figures and — by an entirely different route — arrives at results which are similar in content but entirely different in form.

It would not be far wrong to assume that everything that André Thomkins absorbs is stored and converted into material for the contents and forms of this art. At the same time he mobilizes every technique and every process for continually fresh possibilities of expression.

I cannot think of any technique or process which he has not used as to the manner born. He draws with pencil and crayon, with steel, bamboo or quill pen, he paints with the brush — in water, oil, or whatever can be bought in the shop. Sometimes he fetches what he needs from the garden: say, a fungus called "inky cap" from which he makes a durable sepia-coloured ink.

Sometimes he revives a forgotten technique — such as the Renaissance drawing highlighted with white. And now and then he finds a new one of his own such as the lackskin or the cardboard intarsia.

Thomkins makes even the size of the picture he selects a determining factor for his art. In the first case he draws under a magnifying glass, with short fingers as you might say; in the second he works from the wrist — which automatically and intentionally leads to different forms of expression through a different ductus.

For André Thomkins everything becomes material and method: the use of language, the exploration of material à l'état brut, techniques, processes — and something else: mixing with people.

I know of no other artist who has so persistently sought collaboration with other artists. The works he has done at the suggestion or instance of Daniel Spoerri make up a complete "oeuvre" of their own — from "shadowbuttonegg" to the unfinished "Darmrad". But also Dieter Rot, Franz Eggenschwiler, Jean Tinguely, Bernhard Luginbühl, Robert Filliou, Konrad Klaphek, Horst Jansen, Constant, François Morellet, Ray Johnson and many, many others might be cited as partners in his work.

Just as with his choice assortment of books, his choice of friends is also select. No stranger, came he from never so remote a star, would remain strange to him for long.

Seeing things like this, one must ask: Is there anything or anyone André Thomkins cannot turn into a method? — I don't know. I cannot imagine anything or anyone that escapes André Thomkins once he or it has become the focus of his mind.

It would be true to say: André Thomkins is the most radical, indeed, the out-and-out methodist — and yet there is, in spite of the dizzy abundance of what his inspiration has produced — a common denominator for everything. And that is: he invariably arrives via the material at his method and from there goes on to art — from outside inwards, that is.

What was and is so pleasing for me is: that André Thomkins is, as it were, complementary to me. With me everything is the other way round: I work from inside outwards. I begin with art, with the idea of what I want to realize; and then I look for the methods and materials.

And the most gratifying aspect of all is: that precisely the knowledge of this complementarity continually replenishes my courage to go on with my work with the same radicality as André Thomkins goes on with his.

In an early opus — "L'âme de Victor Hugo" — Raymond Roussel represents the soul of the author as a noisy, stuffy, steamy restless engine-room of a factory in which — as in Adolf Menzel's rolling mill — ideas are produced and sentences wrought under high pressure. I see André Thomkins's mind rather as a Garden of Earthly Delights where everything André Thomkins has perceived, stored in his unconscious and admitted to his conscious mind thrives and grows.

I can imagine that Hieronymous Bosch, perhaps also Hans Robiscek and Justinus Kerner and perhaps many, many more would go on picking the fruit and boiling the peel there for ever more; and the vapours would rise beneficently to André Thomkins's head; and from there—thank God—set his hand in motion through a hermetic mutation. Which would show that André Thomkins is not a methodist after all.

Karl Gerstner

(Translation: D. Q. Stephenson)

Biography

Born 1930 in Lucerne.

Grammar-school. Art-school, taught by Max von Moos.

Friendship with Serge Stauffer.

Interest in Dada.

1950/51 Paris, some Croquis-drawing at Grande Caumière.

1952 marries Eva Schnell, moves to Rheydt, where Eva lives, painting and teaching art.

1954 moves to Essen, where his family has lived since.

1955 Lacquer-paintings, "Lachskins", newly invented technique (shown at Gallery van den Loo in Essen 1960/61 and 1970 in exhibition "Der Bildungstrieb der Stoffe" at the Nürnberg Kunsthalle. Description of the technique in their catalogue).

1956 Interpreted overdrawn newspaper-illustrations.

Meets Daniel Spoerri in Bern.

1957 Takes part in exhibition "Malende Dichter — Dichtende Maler" at Kunstmuseum St. Gallen.

September: first palindromes (groups of words equally legible back to front).

1962 "Mühlenbild".

1966—1967 Stained-glas windows for the protestant church in Sursee (CH).

1969 First large exhibition at Gallery Handschin, Basle.

1971 Exhibition at Kunstmuseum Basle: "Zeichnungen — Paraphrasen";
Eat-Art at Spoerri's Gallery in Düsseldorf; "Lucerne en Recul", at Gallery Raeber, Lucerne.

1971—1973 Professorship for painting at the Art Academy Düsseldorf.

1973 first Oeuvre catalogue and exhibition at Städt. Museum, Leverkusen; Kunstverein Braunschweig and Museum der Stadt Solothurn.

1977 Complete graphics catalogue published by Edition Stähli, Zürich.

1978 Travelling exhibition: Gemeentemuseum, The Hague; Nijmeegs-Museum, Nijmeegen; Kunsthalle Düsseldorf; Kunsthalle Tübingen; Mannheimer Kunstverein; etc.

Exhibition "Lucul", Oeuvre 1946—1978, Kunstmuseum Luzern.

Bibliography

1954 „Schri-Kunst-schri", Kalender, Woldemar Klein, Verlag, Baden-Baden.
1958 „Permanentszene", in: Das neue Forum 9, hrsg. G. R. Sellner, Verlag
Stichnote, Darmstadt.
1960 „Permanentszene", in: Movens, hrsg. Franz Mon, Wiesbaden; „A. T.",
in: Nota 4, hrsg. J. Morschel, Von Graevenitz, München. 1961 Internationale
Manuskriptenausstellung, Konkrete Poesie, Wuppertal.
1962 Daniel Spoerri, „Topographie anecdotée du hasard", Ed. Galerie Lawrence,
Paris.
1963 „Oh! cet écho!", Selbstverlag, Essen; J. A. Thwaites, „Pictures on Exhibit",
New York.
1965 Carlheinz Caspari, „Initionsrede eines Seiltänzers" (ill.), Olefer Hagar-
presse, Schleiden.
1966 Daniel Spoerri, „An anecdoted Topography of Chance", Something Else
Press, New York; „A. T.", in: Stahl und Form, Verlag Stahleisen, Düsseldorf;
„Edition et, 1", Verlag Grutzmacher, Berlin.
1967 „A. T.", in: Fourre Tout, hrsg. Ben Vautier, Nizza; „A. T.", in: Edition et,
3, Verlag Grützmacher, Berlin; Emmett Williams, „An Anthology of Concrete
Poetry", Something Else Press, New York; „A. T.", in: Le petit Colosse de Simi,
hrsg. Daniel Spoerri, Simi (Gr.); André Thomkins, „Schwebzeile" Rolf Kuhn
Verlag, Aachen.
1968 „Magie à la noix, Zimtzauberkonserven", Daniel Spoerri, Galerie Gunar,
Düsseldorf; Karl Gerstner, „Programme entwerfen", Verlag Arthur Niggli,
Teufen; André Thomkins, „Futura 25" Edition Hansjörg Mayer, Stuttgart;
„Spoerris Max und Morimal Art", Galerie Felix Handschin, Basel.
1970 Karl Gerstner, „Do-it-your-self Kunst", in: Spiegelschrift 3, Galerie
Der Spiegel, Köln; Daniel Spoerri, „The mythological Travels", Something Else
Press, New York; Daniel Spoerri, „Gastronomisches Tagebuch" (ill.), Luchter-
hand, Neuwied.
1971 „Glasfenster in Sursee", in: Das Werk 5, 1971; „Geschichten Berichte
Gedichte", Hirschgraben Verlag, Frankfurt/M.; Robert Filliou, „A selection from
1000 basic Japanese poems — ein Sublimat aus 1000 Gedichte Japanisch", vert.
A. T., Spiegelschrift 5, Galerie Der Spiegel, Köln; Daniel Spoerri, „Krims Krams
Magie" (ill.), Edition Hansjörg Mayer, Stuttgart—London; Walter Aue, „Pro-
jecte, Concepte, Actionen", Dumont Verlag, Köln; Daniel Spoerri, „Dokumente
zu Krims Krams Magie", Merlin Verlag, Hamburg.
1972 Franz Bächtiger, „Big Cloisters", in: DU, Februar; Wolfgang Bessenich,
„A. T.", in Kunst: 28 Schweizer, Edition Galerie Raeber, Luzern; „A. T."
in: Publikation der Gotthard Bank, Zürich—Lugano.
1973 George Brecht, „Autobiographie", Spiegelschrift 6, Galerie Der Spiegel,

Köln; „A. T.", in: Kunstforum International I, 4/5; Barbara Catoir, „A. T.", in: Das Kunstwerk XXVI, 3; Gerda Benesch, „A. T." in: Das Kunstwerk XXVI, 6.
1975 Peter Winter, „A. T.", in: Das Kunstwerk XXVIII, 1.
1976 „Concrete Poetry from East and West Germany, Yale University Press, New Haven and London, „Zweitschrift", 1, hrsg. U. und M. Erlhoff, Hannover; Kat. Wiegand, Galerie Jean Briance, Paris.
1977 „André Thomkins — Die Druckgraphik und Monotypisches", Edition Stähli, Zürich; „Kreativer Umgang mit Konkreter Poesie", Herder Bücherei; Kat. Mölzer, Kulturgeschichtliches Museum, Osnabrück; Kat. Back Bilder, Kunstverein Hannover; „Reaktion", 1, hrsg. Verlaggalerie, Düsseldorf; „A. T.", „ORDNENS" in: Sondern Nr. 2, Edition am Mehringdamm, Berlin.
1978 „André Thomkins-Permanentszene", Ed. Hansjörg Mayer, Stuttgart; „Thomkins-Journal Nr. 1—3", Kunstmuseum Luzern (zus. mit „Permanent-szene"), Ausstellungskatalog zur Ausstellung André Thomkins (19. 3. bis 23. 4. 1978) im Kunstmuseum Luzern; „Stiftung Anne-Marie und Victor Loeb" Kunsthalle Bern 1970.

Editions

1965 "Dogmat-mot", edition of 111, Ed. Gallery Der Spiegel, Cologne; Ed. Thek, Düsseldorf.
1968 "Zahnschutz gegen Gummiparagraphen", edition unlimited, Vice Versand, Remscheid.
1969 "Rocker", art intermedia, Cologne.
1970 "jung fern heute", edition of 200, Ed. Tangente, Heidelberg.
1971 "Dogma: I am God", Eat Art Gallery, Düsseldorf.
"Whit Spaghetti genudelte Macroni", edition of 30, Eat Art Gallery, Düsseldorf.
"Lucerne en recul", Gallery Raeber, Lucerne, edition of 100.

One-man shows

1960 Galerie van den Loo, Essen; „Lackskinpresentation", Institution of Contemporary Art, London.

1963 Galerie Bel Etage, Zürich; Büro Gerstner, Gredinger und Kutter, Basel; »Regelbarer Ableger«, Ambulanz-Galerie Schneider-Wesseling, Köln.

1964 Maison des Beaux-Arts, Paris; Pianohaus Kohl, Gelsenkirchen.

1965 Haus van der Grinten, Kranenburg; Kunstkreis Bottrop.

1966 Galerie Schütz, Bad Godesberg.

1967 Saba-Studio, Villingen.

1968 Galerie Hansjörg Mayer, Stuttgart; Galerie Ubu, Karlsruhe.

1969 Galerie Hete Hünermann, Rolandseck; Galerie art intermedia, Köln; Felix Handschin, Basel (Kat.).

1971 Neue Galerie, Baden-Baden; „Lucerne en recul", Galerie Raeber, Luzern (Kat.); „Zeichnungen — Paraphrasen", Kunstmuseum Basel (Kat.).

1972 Galerie Dorothea Leonhart, München (Kat.); Galerie im Taxi-Palais, Innsbruck (Kat.).

1973 „Palindromen en aanvullingen". Galerie im Goethe-Institut / Provisorium, Amsterdam; Städtisches Museum, Leverkusen (Kat.); Kunstverein Braunschweig e. V.; Museum der Stadt Solothurn (Kat.).

1974 Galerie Stähli, Zürich; Galerie Meyer-Ellinger, Frankfurt; Kestner Gesellschaft, Hannover (Kat.); Galerie Gunter Sachs, Hamburg.

1975 Galerie Stähli, Zürich.

1976 Galerie Oben, Hagen.

1977 „Die gesamte Druckgrafik", Kunstmuseum Basel; Galerie Stähli, Zürich.

1978 „Permanentszene", Gemeentemuseum, Den Haag; Nijmeegs Museum Nijmeegen; Kunsthalle, Düsseldorf; „Lucul", Werkübersicht 1946—1978, Kunstmuseum Luzern (Kat.); Galerie Marika Malacorda, Genève; „Die gesamte Druckgrafik", Folkwang-Museum, Essen, Kunstmuseum St. Gallen, Kunstmuseum Kassel.

1957 „Dichtende Maler — Malende Dichter", Kunstmuseum St. Gallen (Kat.).
1962 „Mini-Collages", Galerie St. Laurent, Brüssel; Institute of Contemporary
Art, London.
1965 „Table des Matières", Galerie Ursula Girardon, Paris; „Edition
MAT/MAT-MOT", Galerie der Spiegel, Köln; Galerie Zwirner, Köln.
1966 Galerie Aktuell, Berlin; Galerie Ziegler; Librairie La Hune, Paris;
„Labyrinthe", Akademie der Künste, Berlin, Kunsthalle Baden-Baden,
Kunsthalle Nürnberg (Kat.).
1967 „Möglichkeiten auf Papier", Galerie Heide Hildebrand, Klagenfurt.
1968 „Edition Hansjörg Mayer", Haags Gemeentemuseum, Den Haag (Kat.);
„Science Fiction", Kunsthalle Düsseldorf (Kat.).
1969 Fründ Friends Freunde und Freunde", Kunsthalle Bern, Kunsthalle
Düsseldorf (Kat.); „Attitüden", Galerie Felix Handschin, Basel (Kat.);
„Intermedia '69", Heidelberg (Kat.); „Phantastische Figuration", Helmhaus
Zürich.
1970 „Der Bildungstrieb der Stoffe", Kunsthalle Nürnberg (Kat.); „Jetzt",
Kunsthalle Köln (Kat.); „Text", Buchstabe, Bild", Helmhaus, Zürich (Kat.);
„Strategy: get arts", International Festival, Edinburgh (Kat.); „3—00",
„New Multiple Art", Whitechapel Art Gallery, London; „Multiple Markt",
Kaufhof am Welvehaus, Düsseldorf.
1971 „? konkrete poëzie", Stedlijk Museum, Amsterdam, Kunstverein Stuttgart
(Kat.); „In Memoriam Friends", Eat Art Galerie, Düsseldorf; „Schweizer
Zeichnungen im 20. Jahrhundert", Staatliche Graphische Sammlungen, München,
Winterthur, Bern, Genève (Kat.); „Les Passe-partout", Galerie Ben Doute
de Tout, Nizza (Kat.); Düsseldorf, „Stadt der Künstler", Vortragszentrum der
Neuen Messe, Düsseldorf-Stockum; „Damen-Friseur", Co-op Galerie,
Düsseldorf.
1972 „Grenzgebiet der Bildenden Kunst", Staatsgalerie Stuttgart;
„Metamorphose des Dinges", Kunsthalle, Basel; 31 Artistes Suisses Contem-
porians", Galeries Nationales du Grand Palais, Paris; „Documenta 5", Kassel;
„Die Handzeichnung der Gegenwart", Kunsthaus Zürich; „Karikaturen?",
Kunsthaus Zürich; „Avantguardia Svizzera", Rotonda di Via Basani, Milano
(Kat.); „Amsterdam—Paris—Düsseldorf"; Guggenheim Museum, New York,
Pasadena Art Museum, Museum of Fine Art, Dallas; „Marcel Broodthaers,
„Der Adler vom Oligozän bis heute", Kunsthalle Düsseldorf.
1973 „Bilanz einer Aktivität", Galerie im Goethe Institut / Provisorium,
Amsterdam; „Stuttgarter Museumsbesitz", Kunstmuseum Zürich; „Profile",
Kunstsammlung Bochum; „Idole", Aktionsgalerie, Bern.
1974 „Surrealität — Bildrealität 1924—1974", Kunsthalle Düsseldorf, Kunsthalle

Baden-Baden (Kat.); „Gegenwart VII — Druckgraphik der Schweiz", Städte-bund-Ausstellungen des Kunstvereins für die Rheinlande und Westfalen.
1975 „18 Deutsche Zeichner", Kunsthalle Baden-Baden; „Kunst fürs Büro", Rheinisches Museumsamt, Bonn; „Jeunes graveurs Suisses, Paris.
1976 „Trait pour trait", Galerie Jean Briance, Paris; „Junggesellenmaschinen", Kunsthalle Düsseldorf, Stedelijk Museum Amsterdam; „Robert Filliou et André Thomkins, Pantogrammes", Galerie Felix Handschin, Basel; „Present Projects", Edition Leger, Malmö; „Zeichnungen von 10 Schweizer Künstler", Kunsthaus Zürich; „Bis Heute, Zeichnungen aus dem Karl A. Burckhardt-Koechlin-Fonds", Kunsthalle, Basel; Galerie Marika Malacorda, Genève.
1977 „Die Reise nach Amsterdam", Verlaggalerie Leaman, Köln; „The museum of Drawers, Herbert Distels Schubladen Museum", Kunstmuseum Solothurn, Kunsthalle Düsseldorf; „Städtische Kunsthalle Düsseldorf 1967—1977", Kunst-halle Düsseldorf; „Documenta 6", Kassel; „Daniel Spoerri's Boutique Aberrante", Centre Beaubourg, Paris; „Arnold Böcklin", Kunstmuseum Basel.
1978 „Stiftung Anne-Marie und Victor Loeb", Kunsthalle Bern.